# Understanding Xi Jinping's
## Educational Philosophy

# 习近平总书记
# 教育重要论述讲义

外语教学与研究出版社
FOREIGN LANGUAGE TEACHING AND RESEARCH PRESS
北京 BEIJING

高等教育出版社·北京
HIGHER EDUCATION PRESS   BEIJING

**图书在版编目（CIP）数据**

习近平总书记教育重要论述讲义 ＝ Understanding Xi Jinping's Educational
Philosophy：英文／本书编写组编；英文翻译组译. —— 北京：外语教学与研究
出版社：高等教育出版社，2022.5（2022.10 重印）
ISBN 978-7-5213-3595-8

Ⅰ. ①习… Ⅱ. ①本… ②英… Ⅲ. ①习近平－讲话－学习参考资料－英文
②教育事业－中国－学习参考资料－英文 Ⅳ. ①D2-0②G52

中国版本图书馆 CIP 数据核字 (2022) 第 077563 号

出 版 人　王　芳
责任编辑　仲志兰
责任校对　易　璐
装帧设计　高　蕾
出版发行　外语教学与研究出版社
社　　址　北京市西三环北路 19 号（100089）
网　　址　http://www.fltrp.com
印　　刷　北京华联印刷有限公司
开　　本　787×1092　1/16
印　　张　14.5
版　　次　2022 年 8 月第 1 版 2022 年 10 月第 2 次印刷
书　　号　ISBN 978-7-5213-3595-8
定　　价　70.00 元

购书咨询：（010）88819926　电子邮箱：club@fltrp.com
外研书店：https://waiyants.tmall.com
凡印刷、装订质量问题，请联系我社印制部
联系电话：（010）61207896　电子邮箱：zhijian@fltrp.com
凡侵权、盗版书籍线索，请联系我社法律事务部
举报电话：（010）88817519　电子邮箱：banquan@fltrp.com
物料号：335950001

记载人类文明
沟通世界文化
www.fltrp.com

## Compilation Team

**Team Leader**
Yang Xiaohui

**Team Members (in alphabetical order)**

| | | |
|---|---|---|
| Ai Silin | Fan Guorui | Gao Deyi |
| Pang Lisheng | Qin Xuan | Shen Wenhua |
| Shi Zhongying | Sun Xiguo | Wan Meirong |
| Wang Binglin | Wang Zhanren | Yang Yinfu |
| Yang Zhaoshan | Zhai Xiaoning | Zhang Qingshou |

## Translation Team

**Team Leader**
Ren Wen

**Team Members**

| | | |
|---|---|---|
| Li Changshuan | Peng Ping | Tham Wai Mun |
| Zhai Zheng | Zhu Yuben | Liu Yubo |
| Liu Moxiao | Eliot I. Wycoff | |

**English Language Editor**
David W. Ferguson

**Xi Jinping Speaking at the 2018 National Education Conference**

The CPC Central Committee, with General Secretary Xi Jinping at the core, is committed to modernizing education and making it a strategic priority for the country. To this end, it has formulated a set of key policies, major plans, and new concepts, ideas, and perspectives. This photo shows Xi Jinping delivering a keynote speech at the National Education Conference held in Beijing on September 10, 2018.

### Strengthening MPT Courses

The Party and the state attach great importance to the moral and political education of young people, whose healthy growth has been the theme of many speeches made by General Secretary Xi Jinping. In these speeches, he has set out clear requirements for moral and political work in schools, as well as for the development of moral and political theory (MPT) courses. Since the 18th CPC National Congress in 2012, the MPT courses have been steadily reinforced through improvement and innovation. Moral education at secondary and primary schools and universities has been better coordinated. This photo, taken on March 18, 2019, shows Xi Jinping chairing a meeting with MPT teachers in the Great Hall of the People. At the meeting, he emphasized the need to cultivate in students a firm belief in socialism with Chinese characteristics for a new era, to implement the Party's education policy, and to accomplish the fundamental task of building strong moral character.

## Xi Jinping Attending to the Education of Children

Xi Jinping pays special attention to the development of children, emphasizing that the next generation must receive a good education. This photo shows him with a group of children at Beijing Children's Palace on May 29, 2013, shortly before International Children's Day.

## Illuminating the Future of Humanity with Mutual Learning Among Civilizations

Exchange and mutual learning make civilizations richer and more colorful. The year 2019 marked the fifth anniversary of President Xi Jinping's speech at the UNESCO headquarters. Over the years, he has traveled from the Seine to the Nile, from the Ural Mountains to the Andes, to build bridges between China and the rest of the world. He has demonstrated the importance of mutual learning and disseminated the concept of "mutual appreciation and common prosperity." This photo shows Xi Jinping delivering a speech at the UNESCO headquarters in Paris on March 27, 2014.

## Technical and Vocational Education Contributing to Targeted Poverty Alleviation

To help poor families and give everyone opportunities to find employment and excel, the state has formulated an important education strategy that aims at developing technical and vocational education in less developed and rural areas, helping children from poor families acquire technical skills, and eradicating poverty through education. This photo shows Xi Jinping talking with teachers and students while observing a vocational skills training session in the Modern Manufacturing Technology Training Room at Shandan Bailie School, Zhangye city, Gansu province, on August 20, 2019.

## Xi Jinping Attaching Great Importance to Building a Body of Qualified Teachers

Since the 18th CPC National Congress, the CPC Central Committee with Xi Jinping at the core has attached great importance to building a body of qualified teachers, calling for the strengthening of their professional ethics and integrity while valuing teachers and education. In November 2017, Xi Jinping presided over the first meeting of the 19th Central Leading Group for Deepening Reform. At the meeting, the Group reviewed and approved Guidelines on Deepening Reform to Build a Body of Qualified Teachers in the New Era, the first milestone policy document of its kind adopted by the CPC since the founding of the People's Republic of China. This photo shows Xi Jinping meeting representatives of outstanding educational institutions and teachers honored on the thirtieth Teachers' Day in the Great Hall of the People on September 9, 2014.

# Contents

# Introduction

## Guidelines for an Educational Powerhouse in the New Era

Since the 18th National Congress of the Communist Party of China (CPC) in 2012, General Secretary Xi Jinping has led the whole Party and people of all ethnic groups in advancing the great cause of the Party and the state. In this process, he has made a series of key statements on education reform and development in light of a shifting global landscape, national development goals, and the Chinese Dream of national rejuvenation. These statements focus on the fundamental questions of what kind of talent should be trained, how, and for whom, and define the fundamental mission of education as building strong moral character. Xi Jinping's educational philosophy, an integral part of Xi Jinping Thought on Socialism with Chinese Characteristics for a New Era, is the latest achievement in applying the basic principles of Marxism to education in China, and it represents a new height reached by the Party in understanding education. In addition, it points the way for socialist education in China and prescribes the foundational principles for the reform and development of education in the new era.

# 1. The Background of Xi Jinping's Educational Philosophy

"What keeps a pond as clear as a mirrored sky? The fount is where its waters never run dry."[1] Following the 18th CPC National Congress, General Secretary Xi Jinping visited many nurseries, kindergartens, elementary schools, secondary schools, technical and vocational institutes, and higher education institutions to convey the great importance that he attached to education, and to emphasize the need to nurture new generations to carry on the socialist cause. He held forums with educational institutions and replied to letters from students and teachers on this subject. He presided over a series of meetings with the Standing Committee of the Political Bureau of the CPC Central Committee, the Political Bureau of the CPC Central Committee, the Central Leading Group for Deepening Reform, and the Central Commission for Deepening Reform, which deliberated and adopted a catalogue of programs in the field of education, and put forward major proposals on education reform and development. The CPC Central Committee then hosted the first National Education Conference in the new era on September 10, 2018. In his keynote speech, General Secretary Xi expounded on the fresh ideas, perspectives, and concepts derived from the country's education reform and development. The conference celebrated a milestone in education reform in China, and launched a new drive to accelerate education modernization, make the country an

---

1 Cited from a poem by Zhu Xi (1130-1200), a preeminent scholar and thinker of the Southern Song dynasty (1127-1279), who contributed to giving Confucian teachings new relevance.

educational powerhouse, and ensure that education meets the expectations of the people.

Xi Jinping's educational philosophy is based on his insight into the world's development trends and his understanding of global shifts in the educational landscape. The world is undergoing another round of extensive recalibration, transformation, and development, but peace and development remain the themes of our times. Multipolarity in international relations, economic globalization, IT application, and cultural diversity are increasing the socio-economic interconnectedness and interdependence of countries, and the transformation of global governance mechanisms and international order is accelerating. A new wave of technological and industrial revolution is reconfiguring the landscape of global innovation, and in particular the international economic framework. Life-changing modern technologies—exemplified by the Internet, big data, cloud computing, satellite-based quantum communications, and artificial intelligence—are profoundly impacting the ways of living, working, learning, and thinking. The competition in overall national strength grows fiercer by the day. Against this backdrop, the fight for global talent and the nurturing of domestic talent have come under the spotlight. Finding ways to remodel the education system for the modern age and to nurture creative talent pools to meet the tests of our times has become humanity's new challenge. Likewise, a tide of revolution is brewing in the sphere of global education. Calls for education reform commensurate with socio-economic development have marked the rise of learner-centered education, learning for competence, and all-round development of the individual. Similarly, more people are embracing the ideas of learning for all, lifelong learning, and personalized learning. Educational models, practices, teaching content, and learning styles are undergoing a makeover, as educational governance is evolving toward multiparty cooperation and extensive participation. Meanwhile, in the field of global education, progress has been achieved in ensuring inclusive and equitable quality education, and promoting lifelong learning opportunities for all.

Xi Jinping's educational philosophy is founded against a backdrop in which Chinese socialism enters a new era and education in China takes on new missions and tasks. The CPC Central Committee with General Secretary Xi Jinping at the core has acted with great political courage and a strong sense of responsibility to overcome great challenges, move forward on great projects, undertake great causes, and realize great dreams. Many long-standing problems have been resolved, and much has been accomplished. A series of historic reforms have been undertaken, ushering in a new era for socialism with Chinese characteristics. The era is new in four respects. First, it marks China's entrance into a new stage of development: the nation has stood up and become prosperous, and it is now growing in strength. Second, it marks the theoretical innovations of the Communist Party of China and localization of Marxism in China to stay abreast with the times. Third, it marks the changing of the principal challenge facing Chinese society—how to fill the gap between unbalanced and inadequate development and the people's ever-growing expectation of a better life. Fourth, it marks the new goal we are moving toward: as we are about to secure a decisive victory in building a moderately prosperous society in all respects, we are also ready to embark on a new journey to fully build a modern socialist China.

As China marches forward, our demand for scientific knowledge and exceptional talent will intensify in parallel with our expectations for equitable and higher quality education. Making education a basic necessity, fulfilling its demonstrative role, and adopting a whole-system approach are obvious imperatives. Entering this new era, China is moving to the fore as an innovative country. Thus, we need a future-ready education program that can nurture a new generation of highly adaptable and innovative talent that enables China's strategic transformation from a follower to a competitor, and then a pacesetter in science and technology. Entering this new era, China is sprinting to become an economic power. Education will serve this purpose by developing the appropriate human and talent resources and by providing a constant impetus to transform China's economy from one that is factor- and investment-driven to one that is driven by innovation. Entering this new era, China will challenge itself to develop a great socialist culture. This objective will prime our education programs to be founded on an unswerving commitment to understand and practice the core socialist values. In addition, our education system must inherit and pass on China's splendid cultural heritage, and continue to enrich its soft power while learning from other civilizations. Entering this new era, China endeavors to build a community with a shared future for humanity. To this end, our education programs will promote exchanges between peoples, countries, and civilizations. China will thus contribute to a brighter future for humanity in new and greater ways.

In accordance with the development trend outlined above, Xi Jinping's educational philosophy comprehensively summarizes China's experience in education reform and development, with a focus on solving real-world problems. Education remains the prime concern of the CPC and the state. From the founding of the People's Republic of China in 1949, through reform and opening up in 1978, to the present day, the great strides made in reforming and developing China's education have attracted worldwide attention. In establishing the world's largest education system, China has blazed new trails in developing socialist education, which has contributed significantly to its economic and social growth. Since the 18th CPC National Congress, the CPC Central Committee with General Secretary Xi Jinping at the core has implemented the strategy of rejuvenating the country through science, education, and talent pooling. It has given priority to educational development through reform, investment, and modernization efforts, and has sought to raise education to a new level. The CPC leadership in education has never been stronger, nor has moral and political education in schools been keener. The impact has been significant: students have a stronger moral framework, and stakeholders in education have a stronger sense of confidence. There has also been considerable growth in the quality and standards of school operation—in basic education, technical and vocational education, higher education, and various other forms of educational undertakings. In addition, the teaching workforce—especially in rural areas—has also been given more support through an ongoing effort to raise the political, social, and professional status of teachers. To remedy shortcomings in education, a comprehensive scheme has been implemented to aid financially challenged students at all levels. These markers of significant progress in education equity have bolstered the populace's sense of gain.

China has launched a number of major educational reform initiatives and made considerable breakthroughs in solving deep-rooted and fundamental issues in education. To this end, the steady elevation in standards and the expansion of educational openness have lifted China's influence in global education to the extent that its overall standards of education are now at the upper middle level of the world. The next phase of work will focus on improving quality, optimizing structures, and promoting equity. Our achievements to date should not, however, cloud our sober recognition that education provision in the country is far from balanced and adequate, nor is it commensurate with the increased requirements for national economic and social growth or the expectations of the people. First, there is a need to establish a rational and scientific base for educational development, to ensure character education, to further strengthen moral and political education, and to increase the quality of the teaching workforce to fulfil the needs of modern education. Second, the noticeable gaps in educational development between different regions and between urban and rural areas must be plugged, and the provision of basic public education services should be standardized across the board. Third, compulsory education in rural areas, pre-school education, and technical and vocational education remain inadequate, and the institutional mechanisms for effectively managing lifelong learning for all remain to be improved. Fourth, talent training provisions need to adapt to changing social needs, and the capacity of education to drive innovation and pivot the general opening up of China must expand. Fifth, the mechanism of government-led investment in education with social participation has much room for improvement, and China's capacity for governance in education must be modernized.

## 2. The Content of Xi Jinping's Educational Philosophy

In this age of rapid change, the extent of our practice and degree of our development have a direct bearing on our breadth of mind in theoretical innovation. General Secretary Xi has focused on the fundamental questions of what kind of people should be trained, how, and for whom, and he is seeking solutions anchored in the Two Centenary Goals[1] and the Chinese Dream of national rejuvenation. These solutions must keep China on the path of Chinese socialist education, and prepare new generations to carry on the socialist cause—such individuals shall be morally, intellectually, physically, and aesthetically developed with a love for labor. At the National Education Conference in 2018, Xi Jinping introduced new concepts, ideas, and perspectives on education reform and development based on our practice.

First, we must adhere to the CPC leadership over education. The leadership of the Party breeds success in all Chinese affairs. The Party must firmly maintain its leadership over education. It must hold fast to the guidance of Marxism and link the complete management processes of educational institutions with moral and political education while increasing its presence within the education system.

Second, we must stay true to the fundamental mission of building moral character. Moral integrity concerns the future of our Party and our nation. It must be the criterion against which we measure all educational activities. We must train our students to have strong morals, and create a ready pool of new generations of socialist builders who are developed morally, intellectually, physically, aesthetically, and with a love for labor to shoulder the responsibility of national rejuvenation.

---

1 The first is to achieve the goal of "building a moderately prosperous society in all respects" in 2021 when the CPC celebrates its centenary. The second is to achieve the goal of "building a modern socialist country that is prosperous, strong, democratic, culturally advanced, and harmonious" in 2049 when China celebrates its 100th anniversary.

Third, we must prioritize education. Education is a major undertaking of the state and the Party. A nation prospers when its education system flourishes. We must give strategic priority to education to push forward the different undertakings of the Party and the state, and highlight the fundamental, pioneering, and holistic role of education.

Fourth, we must keep to the path of socialist education. China is a socialist country led by the CPC; as such, it advocates socialist education and stands firm on this path. We maintain that education must serve the people, serve the CPC in the governance of the country, serve the objectives of consolidating and developing Chinese socialist institutions, serve the objectives of reform and opening up, and serve the modernization of socialism.

Fifth, we must insist on running education with a firm footing within China. Education in China must reflect the unique characteristics of China and be adapted to the country's context. It has to be rooted in China while building bridges connecting with foreign lands, and it must keep abreast with the times and be forward-looking. With this in mind, we must strive to build a world-class, modern education system.

Sixth, we must maintain a people-centered approach throughout educational development. Education equity is a cornerstone of social equity. We must make sure that benefits of educational development be shared among the people in a more equitable manner as part of our effort to promote social equity and justice. We must strive to ensure equal access to education for all, empowering all to grow and develop, and encouraging all to contribute to society and bring benefits to the people.

Seventh, we must drive deeper education reform and innovation. Reform is the fundamental driving force behind educational endeavors. We must take a systematic, holistic, and coordinated approach to education reform which instills vigor and vitality into educational undertakings. And we must deal with major problems and urgent issues in a timely manner.

Eighth, we must uphold the key mission of education to contribute to the great rejuvenation of the Chinese nation. To accomplish the Two Centenary Goals and realize the Chinese Dream of national rejuvenation, we must depend on talent and education. In pushing for the quality development of education and in expanding the capacity of education suited to social and economic growth, it is necessary to formulate a holistic approach to promoting the Five-Sphere Integrated Plan[1] and the Four-Pronged Comprehensive Strategy[2].

Ninth, we must lay the proper groundwork by building up the teaching workforce. Teaching staff underpin a robust education system and determine the impact that education can make. Strengthening the teaching workforce is of strategic significance. To this end, the primary yardstick of a quality teaching workforce has to be professional ethics and integrity. Specifically, a highly professional quality teaching workforce must embrace the elements of lofty ideals, moral integrity, knowledge, and compassion.

Xi Jinping's educational philosophy cuts to the heart of key challenges in developing a unique Chinese socialist education. It points the way for directional, fundamental, whole-system, and strategic issues. It demonstrates a deep understanding of China's educational undertakings. We should remain focused on these hard-won insights, and progressively enrich and develop them.

A good theory must be well-grounded in practice, answer the questions of the times, and meet the needs of the people; it will shine with wisdom and rationality, and resonate with the power of truth. As guidelines for the reform and development of education in China in the new era, Xi Jinping's educational philosophy embodies the educational ideals, concepts, and pursuit of the Chinese communists, and fully demonstrates his profound grasp of the laws of educational development and his commitment to rejuvenate China through education.

General Secretary Xi's educational philosophy expresses the commitment to putting people first. As a saying goes, "Bringing benefits to

---

1 The Five-Sphere Integrated Plan is to promote coordinated economic, political, cultural, social, and ecological advancement.
2 The Four-Pronged Comprehensive Strategy is to make comprehensive moves to finish building a moderately prosperous society in all respects, deepen reform, advance law-based governance, and strengthen Party self-governance.

the people is a constant principle of state governance." He has pointed out, "Standing on the people's side represents the fundamental political stance of the CPC, and it is what distinguishes a Marxist political party from other political parties."[1] His philosophy puts the people at the center of all development and deals with the practical issues that matter most to the people in meeting their educational expectations, fulfilling their growing demands for a better life, and offering every child equal access to quality education. It also encapsulates the materialist conception of history that it is people who create history and the idea of people-centered development, and manifests the fundamental objective of the CPC—to serve the people wholeheartedly.

The educational philosophy presented by Xi Jinping reflects the scientific spirit of seeking truth from facts. It advises that planning and operation must respect realities so that honest decisions may be made and ideas, policies, and programs may be formulated to best fit the circumstances, complying with objective laws and the spirit of science. It is rooted in the national reality of socialism in its initial stage and based on the scientific judgment that socialism with Chinese characteristics has entered a new era. It captures the links within and between educational development, technological revolution, industrial transformation, and competition in overall national strength in today's world. It reveals transformative trends shaping reform and development of Chinese socialist education and illustrates the scientific elements behind how modern education in China shall respect Chinese characteristics yet be comparable to the world's best. Ultimately, it embodies the scientific spirit of Marxism in pursuit of truth, and the pragmatic attitude of the Communist Party of China.

Xi Jinping's educational philosophy demonstrates the richness of Chinese cultural heritage. He has emphasized that, as the soul of a country and a nation, a burgeoning culture helps a country to thrive, and cultural strength raises a nation into greatness. A strong confidence

---

1 Xi Jinping: "Speech at a Ceremony Marking the 95th Anniversary of the Founding of the Communist Party of China," *Qiushi Journal*, October-December 2016, p. 13.

in Chinese culture will bring cultural renaissance to China and support the country's rejuvenation. Rooted in the finest Chinese traditions of respecting culture and education, his expositions are endowed with time-honored classical educational thoughts, such as the following: "The Great Learning consists in manifesting one's illustrious virtue, fulfilling the expectations of the people, and engaging in the endless pursuit of moral perfection."[1] "Teachers with great learning are aplenty, whereas teachers with moral integrity are hard to come by."[2] "Talents are supportive of virtues, and virtues are guidance to talents."[3] "The right approach to loving your children is to guide them to the right path."[4] These age-old maxims have been imbued with new meanings and given new forms of expression in the new era. This reflects the creative transformation and innovation of traditional Chinese philosophy on education, and manifests the heightened awareness and confidence of the CPC in inheriting and carrying forward traditional Chinese culture.

Xi Jinping's philosophy on education exhibits far-sighted, strategic thinking. An everlasting cause grows out of great strategies and wisdom. General Secretary Xi has underlined strategic issues as the pivot to greatness that any political party and country can achieve. Where strategic judgment is accurate and strategic planning is aligned with development trends, the proactive execution of the strategy provides the route to a bright future for both the Party and the people. In light of the Two Centenary Goals and global trends in education and to advance the Five-Sphere Integrated Plan and the Four-Pronged Comprehensive Strategy, Xi Jinping's philosophy provides a strategy and a grand blueprint for education reform and development in the new era, and

---

1 The opening line of *The Great Learning*, a Confucian classic.
2 Cited from *The Book of Zhou*. It was compiled by the Tang-dynasty (618-907) historian Linghu Defen (583-666) and records the official history of the Northern Zhou dynasty (557-581).
3 Cited from *History as a Mirror* by Sima Guang (1019-1086), a scholar of the Northern Song dynasty (960-1127). This monumental piece, first published in 1084, discusses Chinese history from 403 BC to 959 AD.
4 Zuo Qiuming: *Zuo's Commentary on the Spring and Autumn Annals*, Chinese edition, Zhonghua Book Company, 1987, p. 193.

embodies the boldness of vision, big-picture thinking, and breadth of mind of Chinese communists. It defines a critical issue of our times and represents our pledge to strategically remodel education for the ultimate goal of national rejuvenation.

Xi Jinping's educational philosophy illustrates a mindset that faces challenges creatively. According to Marx, issues are epochal manifestos and the most practical cry expressing the inner state of a particular age. Once issues and challenges emerge, they must be screened, studied, and overcome throughout the process of innovation. Xi Jinping has explained clearly that the key to our Party's triumph over adversity lies in creative practices and theoretical innovation. His philosophy focuses on overcoming prominent obstacles in the path of education reform and development in the new era. It also focuses on advancing major educational innovations in the theory of the CPC, while demonstrating the determination of the CPC to take on challenges, to keep abreast with the times, and to manifest the enterprising spirit of the Marxists throughout reform and innovation.

Xi Jinping's educational philosophy is oriented toward executing our responsibility in socialist education. Sound theory is always distilled from practical experience and is in turn enriched and refined through guided execution. General Secretary Xi has advised: "[W]e need to study and grasp the principle of the dialectical relationship between knowledge and practice, always put practice first, and continue to promote theoretical innovation on the basis of practice." "In line with our changing times and practical development, we must continue to deepen our understanding, draw on past experiences, and achieve theoretical innovation. We must uphold dialectical unity between theoretical guidance and practical exploration, and enable positive interaction between theoretical and practical innovation..."[1] His philosophy summarizes the practical experience gained throughout the course of reforming and developing Chinese socialist education. It will be further

---

1 Xi Jinping: "Dialectical Materialism Is the Worldview and Methodology of Chinese Communists," *Qiushi Journal*, January-March 2019, pp. 9, 10.

enriched and improved in the course of implementation and will increasingly demonstrate its strength and power in pushing forward education initiatives.

## 3. The Significance of Xi Jinping's Educational Philosophy

General Secretary Xi Jinping's rich and insightful expositions on education are an important part of Xi Jinping Thought on Socialism with Chinese Characteristics for a New Era, and have important theoretical value and practical significance. They have broken new ground in Marxist educational thought. Marx, Engels, Lenin, and other great thinkers proposed numerous basic principles and important concepts about proletarian education. These concepts, which constitute the basic theoretical framework of Marxist educational thought, may be neatly summed up as follows: that sociality is the essential attribute of education, but education has a class nature in a class-based society; that comprehensive education is necessary for promoting the free and well-rounded development of an individual; and that the only way to bring up a well-rounded individual is to complement education with productive labor. Marxist educational thought has gradually been ingrained with Chinese characteristics by the CPC over the course of leading the Chinese people through revolution, economic development, and reform. Mao Zedong insisted, "Education must serve the politics of the proletariat and must go with productive labor. The working class must increase their level of knowledge, whereas intellectuals must perform manual labor."[1] He also stated, "Our educational policy must enable everyone who receives an education to develop morally, intellectually

---

1 Party Literature Research Office of the CPC Central Committee: *Special Selected Edition of Mao Zedong's Works*, Chinese edition, Central Party Literature Press, Beijing, 2003, p. 1639.

and physically and become a worker with both socialist conscious-ness and culture,"[1] among other important viewpoints. Deng Xiaoping proposed, "Education should be geared to the needs of moderniza-tion, of the world and of the future."[2] He also remarked that we must "encourage all our people to have lofty ideals and moral integrity, to become better educated and to cultivate a strong sense of discipline."[3] Jiang Zemin emphasized the strategy of revitalizing the country through science and education in addition to the strategy of sustainable development. And Hu Jintao made building moral character the funda-mental mission of Chinese socialist education, with the individual at the core of educational development.

Xi Jinping's educational philosophy is reflective regarding the ba-sic positions, viewpoints, and methods of Marxist educational thought. On this basis, it draws further on the uniquely Chinese theoretical in-novation. In so doing, it summarizes China's experience in advancing its socialist education and opens a new chapter in Marxist educational thought. It reiterates the CPC's overall leadership in education, signal-ing that the education system must embody the Party's political will. It advocates cultivating new generations of socialist builders who are well-rounded in moral, intellectual, physical, and aesthetic development and with a love for labor. Highlighting the strategic role of education, it recommends prioritizing the development of education as a proactive strategy to push forward the undertakings of the Party and the state. The emphasis on putting the people at the front and center of the de-velopment of education highlights the value proposition of education, and the emphasis on socialist education grounded in China's unique reality clearly articulates the proper path of development. It proposes to accelerate the pace of development through further improvements,

---

1 Mao Zedong: "On the Correct Handling of Contradictions Among the People," *Selected Works of Mao Zedong*, Vol. V, Foreign Languages Press, Beijing, 1977, p. 405.
2 Deng Xiaoping: "Message Written for Jingshan School," *Selected Works of Deng Xiaoping*, Vol. III, Foreign Languages Press, Beijing, 1994, p. 46.
3 Deng Xiaoping: "Unity Depends on Ideals and Discipline," *Selected Works of Deng Xiaoping*, Vol. III, Foreign Languages Press, Beijing, 1994, p. 116.

reform, and innovation in education. Ultimately it underlines the status and role of teachers by repositioning them as the dream-builders in China's "Dream Team." These novel notions, thoughts, and perspectives, outlined above, provide clarifications to a series of fundamental issues, such as the developmental direction, path, policies, and principles for remaking Chinese socialist education in the new era. They offer a new vision for a deeper understanding of the laws of socialist development, educational advancement, and talent cultivation, marking a new height in the development of educational theories of socialism with Chinese characteristics.

Xi Jinping's philosophy presented in this book has provided guidelines for the modernization of education, the building of an educational powerhouse, and the running of an education system that responds to the expectations of the people. It is the basic guiding principle for what has achieved in education since the 18th CPC National Congress. It has set the strategic objectives and tasks for education reform in the new era and sounded the call to rejuvenate the Chinese nation through education. It has also provided the path and action plan to advance education modernization and make China strong in education. It contains rich theoretical as well as practical approaches to education, expounding what education is, how to understand it, and how to succeed in education. In other words, it provides the boat or bridge for crossing a river.

As we embark on our mission to make China an educational powerhouse in the new era, we must meticulously study and bring into effect the ideas in Xi Jinping's educational philosophy. We must not waver in our beliefs, nor should we evade the historical responsibility of education in the new era, which aims to provide talent and intellectual support for the Two Centenary Goals and the Chinese Dream of national rejuvenation.

# Chapter 1

Overall CPC Leadership
in Education

The Communist Party of China exercises overall leadership in all endeavors across the country. Leadership by the CPC is mandated by history and the people. It is determined by the nature of our state and explicitly provided for in our constitution. CPC leadership is an essential feature and the greatest strength of socialism with Chinese characteristics. General Secretary Xi Jinping has noted that consolidating CPC leadership will deliver success to our education program. Only by upholding the CPC leadership can we promote alignment in thinking, political cohesion, and coordinated action in the realm of education, keep education on the right path, and stick to the course of socialist education with Chinese characteristics.

# 1. Overall Party Leadership for Educational Success

Xi Jinping has always attached importance to our Party leadership over education. During his tenure as secretary of the CPC Zhejiang Provincial Committee (2003-2007), one of his prime concerns was the province's higher education. Within a month of taking office, he visited Zhejiang University Ningbo Institute of Technology (now NingboTech University) to listen to teachers and students, help solve major problems, and steer the school's development. On that occasion, he pointed out that consolidating Party leadership over higher institutions and improving the Party's presence in higher institutions was pivotal for Chinese universities. He drew an analogy between managing a school and managing a province—the key lies in leadership. In July 2004, he attended a meeting where a new secretary of CPC Zhejiang University Committee was appointed. At the meeting, he called on the attendees to uphold and improve the university president responsibility system overseen by the Party Committee, and emphasized that strengthening the leading team was at the heart of the growth of the university. In September 2005, he made the decision to convene a meeting of the Standing Committee of CPC Zhejiang Provincial Committee on the campus of Zhejiang University to focus on developing higher education in the province. Rarely had such a meeting been convened on a university campus. Before the meeting, he visited the university history museum with other participants, reviewing the extraordinary and arduous journey the university had traveled as the fate of the nation was at stake. At the meeting, he set out clear requirements for strengthening Party leadership and moral and political education in higher education institutions—requirements that brought together the thoughts and actions of the Standing Committee of the CPC Zhejiang Provincial Committee and the university leadership.

Speaking at the National Education Conference held in September 2018, Xi Jinping emphasized the need to uphold the overall Party leadership in education. The Communist Party of China, the highest political authority, is the captain steering the cause of socialism with Chinese characteristics. Only the CPC leadership can guarantee the political nature of Chinese socialism. China's education program, serving the largest population in the world, has unbalanced development and noticeable differences in people's expectations. Affirming leadership by the Party is therefore particularly important in maintaining and developing such a complex undertaking.

## 1.1 Commitment to the Four Consciousnesses, the Four-Sphere Confidence, and the Two Upholds

We must maintain political commitment, think in terms of the general picture, follow the core leadership of the CPC Central Committee, and act in accordance with its requirements (the Four Consciousnesses). To uphold the overall Party leadership, we should consciously align ourselves with the CPC Central Committee with Xi Jinping at the core. We must endorse it in our thinking, safeguard it in our political philosophy, comply with it in our organizational arrangements, and follow it in our actions.

To endorse it in our thinking means we must first accurately understand Xi Jinping Thought on Socialism with Chinese Characteristics for a New Era and apply it to examine and clarify issues, assess the situation, analyze problems, and arrive at solutions. We must also apply it to arm our minds, guide our initiatives, and advance our work. To safeguard it in our political philosophy requires us to maintain a high degree of political alert and sensitivity, take a firm political stance, and follow the correct political path. We must be of one heart and one mind with the Central Committee—absolutely loyal and politically reliable. To comply with it in our organizational arrangements, we must place ourselves within the Party organization in all circumstances, keep in mind our obligations and responsibilities as Party members, and trust the Party organization and the Central Committee. To follow it in our actions means we must align ourselves with the Central Committee, adhere to our Party's basic theories, guidelines, and principles, and to the Four Consciousnesses in all aspects of reform, development, and educational and pedagogical research. In this way, we will be able to answer the fundamental questions of what types of talent to train, how, and for whom.

We must raise our confidence in the path, theory, system, and culture of socialism with Chinese characteristics (the Four-Sphere Confidence). Socialism with Chinese characteristics is the only path to realizing socialist modernization, creating a better life for the people, and achieving national rejuvenation. The theory of Chinese socialism, advanced and up-to-date, has proven to be well suited in guiding the Party and the people in rejuvenating the Chinese nation. The Chinese socialist system guarantees national progress with great strengths, and is capable of self-improvement. Chinese socialist culture is the unique feature of the Chinese nation, represents its spiritual pursuit, and motivates the Party and the people to forge ahead. We must apply the Four-Sphere Confidence to running Chinese socialist education, so as to continue to disseminate Marxism, promulgate core socialist values, foster harmony in schools, and cultivate school ethos and academic disciplines. We must educate students to have a proper understanding of the development trends in China and the world, of the unique features of China in the context of the world, of their responsibilities and missions, and of the importance of working to achieve lofty ideals.

We must uphold General Secretary Xi's core position in the CPC Central Committee and in the Party as a whole, and uphold the Central Committee's authority and its centralized, unified leadership (the Two Upholds). As an old adage goes, "While affairs of the state are distributed in localities, major decisions must be taken by the central authority." To uphold and strengthen the overall Party leadership, it is most important to safeguard the authority of the CPC Central Committee and its centralized, unified leadership; to do so, the key is to uphold General Secretary Xi's core position. It is thus imperative to help Party members, officials, faculty, and students reach this understanding from both historical and contemporary, theoretical and practical, and national and international perspectives. In a word, we should continuously enhance our ideological and political consciousness of the Two Upholds, and act accordingly, always keeping in alignment with the CPC Central Committee with Xi Jinping at the core. We should respond positively to what the Central Committee recommends, earnestly implement its decisions, and must not do what it prohibits.

## 1.2 Performing leadership responsibilities

Overall Party leadership over education requires us to improve the Party's capacity and confidence in performing leadership responsibilities, including the resolve and ability to set the direction, control the overall situation, make decisions, build capacity, foster and appoint leaders, and ensure implementation, so as to carry through the Party's guidelines, principles, and policies in schools of all types and at all levels.

---

### ◈ Quote from Xi Jinping ◈

We should uphold the Party leadership over institutions of higher learning and ensure the socialist orientation of schools. We should transform our characteristics and strengths into the capacity to foster new generations of socialist builders.

—Speech at the meeting with teachers and students of Peking University, May 2, 2018

---

*Setting the direction.* Setting a direction is fundamental for overall and long-term development. General Secretary Xi noted that in order to carry out the noble but arduous historic mission and overcome the challenges on the road ahead, it is essential to have our Party in the driver's seat. Party committees at all levels of the education sector should keep steering in the right political direction by implementing the decisions and plans of the CPC Central Committee on reform and development and strengthening Party leadership, fulfilling the responsibility to lead socialist education, and upholding the guidance of Marxism.

*Controlling the overall situation.* Xi Jinping noted that one who fails to plan for the whole is incapable of planning for a part. We must be adept at observing the global picture, identifying problems, and finding solutions specific to the context. Party committees within the education system should consider the overall situation of reform, development, and stability, satisfy immediate needs without losing sight of long-term plans, and solve obvious problems without ignoring deep-seated issues. They should plan and take actions relevant to the circumstances and make their education programs more rational, systematic, and forward-looking.

*Making decisions.* In decision-making, which is of paramount importance, Party committees in the education system should evaluate global, national, and educational factors, as well as the conditions of individual schools. They should not produce subjective or half-baked ideas or break the rules, but should instead improve the relevant procedures and strengthen the rule of law. Decisions and measures should be based on facts and reality, extensive investigation and research; follow scientific, democratic, and law-based procedures; reflect actual situations and objective laws; and can solve real-world problems.

*Building capacity.* The leadership of Party committees is responsible for implementing policies and plans of the CPC Central Committee. Party committees of the education system should build up leadership capacity by improving structures and raising their competence and the quality of their decisions and governance. The leadership should make decisions through democratic centralism in accordance with due procedure. In particular, when it comes to major issues involving finance, projects, and appointment of officials, group consultation should be followed and no one should monopolize the decision. The principal leader in charge of the Party committee should be skillful enough to pool the wisdom of officials at all levels and make sure responsibilities are properly delegated and coordinated. The principal leader should build team unity among the members.

*Fostering and appointing leaders.* Employing capable officials represents the top priority of governance. Party committees should make sure that they select the right leaders. They should strictly abide by the guidelines in appointing leaders and only promote those who are politically reliable, ethical, professionally competent, and enterprising. In fostering and evaluating leaders, they should adopt the criterion of "good officials for the new era." We must make sure that people with the right political orientation are selected and appointed, and that they develop the right work styles and are effectively supervised.

*Ensuring implementation.* The worth of any plan lies in its implementation. Xi Jinping urged that leaders should personally attend to major reform, closely examine each important plan, coordinate key stakeholders, and inspect the results of implementation. Driving a nail with a hammer cannot be done with just one single blow—we must keep hammering until it has been driven home. This is the approach that we must follow. Party committees should focus on taking forceful steps to deliver the various tasks in the entire education reform and development mission, and ensure that the Party's guidelines, principles, and policies in education and the decisions of higher-level Party organizations are carried out to the letter.

## 1.3 Improving institutional mechanisms for overall Party leadership

Overall and strong Party leadership over education is a concrete concept that must be reflected in all aspects of education reform and development.

*Fully implementing the Party's education policy.* The CPC's education policy is the principles and policy statements of the Party and the government on education, providing the fundamental tasks, value orientation, and purposes of education. They set directions and targets, and must be followed. These guidelines are the policy basis for educational decisions, administration, and school activities. General Secretary Xi stated that to implement the Party's education policy in the new era, we should be guided by Marxism and the Thought on Socialism with Chinese Characteristics for a New Era. We should accomplish the fundamental goal of building moral character and molding all-round personalities, and maintain the commitments to serve the people, aid the Party in governance of the country, propel consolidation and development of Chinese socialist institutions, and drive reform and opening up and modernization of China. We should root education in the Chinese soil and combine formal education with productive labor and social practice. We should speed up modernization, establish China's primacy in education, and meet people's expectations for quality education. Our aim is to foster well-rounded individuals committed to the missions of national rejuvenation and socialism.

*Improving the Party's leadership system in education.* We need to plan at the top, understand our stage of development, and identify the path to be taken. We must manage the balance between development needs and our capacity, and between long- and short-term goals. Since the 19th CPC National Congress held in 2017, the Central Committee has further improved the Party's leadership system and formed the Central Leading Group for Education Work. As the coordinating body of the CPC Central Committee for decision-making and deliberation, the group takes as its responsibilities formulating policies for upholding CPC leadership and strengthening CPC presence in the education sector and organizing the implementation of such policies; studying and designing moral and political initiatives in education; reviewing national development strategies, medium- and long-term plans, and major policies and reform programs in education; and facilitating solutions to major problems in education. Establishing the Central Leading Group will support the master-planning and strategic design of education reforms, the modernization of education, and the building of a country strong in education. The move has improved the leadership system by which the Party committee exercises unified leadership, the Party and the administration work hand in hand, and different departments perform designated responsibilities. The setup is of great significance in strengthening the centralized and unified leadership of the CPC Central Committee on education.

*Strengthening the Party's overall management of education.* Xi Jinping pointed out that Party committees must place education on their agenda, and leaders of the Party and the government should be familiar with, care about, and study issues of education. Leading groups in education at the provincial level must ensure that competent government bodies discharge their principal-actor responsibilities. They must strengthen coordination and facilitate the implementation of reform tasks. Local governments at or above the county level should strengthen the supervision of the lower levels of government in performing their education duties. They should pay special attention to urgent issues, difficult problems, and emergencies. As education is a specialized discipline and follows its own law, officials of education departments should respect the laws of education and study relevant issues, seek opinions and suggestions from teachers and experts, and strive to become experts themselves in education management.

*Commitment to the system of president responsibility under the leadership of the Party organization.* This system is the core element of the modern Chinese university system and is fundamental to ensuring Party leadership over universities. It must be upheld and continuously improved. Party committees in universities should exercise overall leadership, including assuming the principal-actor responsibility of governing the Party itself and the university. As the person who supervises all aspects of the Party committee's work, the Party committee secretary bears the main responsibility. The president and other members of the administrative leadership should accept the leadership of the Party committee and implement its decisions. Major issues should be decided by the Party committee through consultation and democratic centralism. Strict standards should be adopted in selecting leaders and deciding on membership of the leading body. It must be ensured that university leadership is assumed by those who are loyal to Marxism, the Party, and the people. It is important to establish Party organizations in all private schools, so that the CPC's education policy is also implemented there. It is also important to improve the principal (dean, director) responsibility system under the leadership of Party organizations in primary and secondary schools and research institutes. In general, schools at all levels must constantly improve their organizational system and working mechanism to ensure that CPC leadership covers all areas of education from top to bottom.

## 2. Moral and Political Education: the Lifeline of All School Work

On March 18, 2019, Xi Jinping hosted a meeting with teachers of moral and political theory (MPT) courses in the Great Hall of the People. It was the first such meeting convened by the CPC Central Committee. Teacher representatives at the meeting felt extremely heartened by the warm atmosphere. Citing his own life experience, Xi Jinping conveyed profound truths in plain words. He offered a penetrating analysis of theoretical and practical issues that troubled teachers. He recalled how emotive his political teacher in junior high school had been when he was recounting the stories of Jiao Yulu, a model CPC county committee secretary, and what a soul-stirring experience it had been for the class. "That lecture had a significant impact on my life, an impact that helped foster my faith," he said. His speech struck a chord with the participants. After the meeting, he shook hands with all the teachers. He gave them a special and unforgettable class on moral and political theory, which demonstrated the importance our Party attaches to moral and political work.

Moral and political work is one of our Party's great traditions and political strengths. It embodies the Party's overall leadership in education, and is instrumental for Party committees in governing the Party itself and running schools. Experience has shown that schools doing well in moral and political work will move forward in the right direction, while those which are lax in or neglect such work will lose their way. In light of the new situation and tasks, moral and political work should always be strengthened and advanced proactively rather than reactively and with confidence in the great struggle for national development, the great project of strengthening our Party, the great cause of Chinese socialism, and the realization of the great dream of national rejuvenation.

---

### ❧ Quote from Xi Jinping ❧

Moral and political education is the lifeline of all work in schools, a lifeline to which all Party committees, education departments, and school Party organizations must hold on.

—Speech at the National Education Conference, September 10, 2018

---

## 2.1 Moral and political work throughout the education process

Moral and political education must be conducted in the entire process of school education, i.e., among all people, and in all processes and dimensions in the realm of education. This requires us to manage both classroom and extracurricular arrangements and both online and offline activities. Moral and political work is by no means the obligation of a single department; it is the responsibility of all and should be integrated into all activities and carried out at all times.

*Consolidating the MPT courses.* Xi Jinping remarked at the 2019 meeting with MPT teachers that MPT courses are fundamental to building moral character. The role of MPT courses is irreplaceable, and the responsibility of teachers great. MPT courses should be strengthened through innovation. He noted that innovation requires us to make courses more thought-provoking, theoretically grounded, attractive, and relevant. Political arguments should be combined with scientific rigor. We should respond to students' questions with thorough analysis, persuade them with well-constructed theory, and guide them with the power of truth. The values promoted should be integrated in knowledge transmission. Criticism should be constructive. Mainstream ideology should be promoted, and misguided views and thoughts challenged. Theory should be tested through practice, particularly in social contexts, in order to nurture lofty ideals and an unyielding spirit in students. We should encourage unity in diversity. While implementing standardized requirements on teaching outcomes, curricula, materials, and management, we should be ready to adapt to local conditions and circumstances and the aptitudes of students. Teachers' guidance and students' independence should be balanced. The guiding and facilitating roles of teachers are indispensable, but it is also necessary to understand students' cognitive process and make them active players in the classroom. Direct teaching should be supplemented by inspiration. Teachers should enlighten students by encouraging them to identify and analyze problems and draw conclusions for themselves. Explicit and implicit instructional approaches should complement each other. Moral and political resources from other courses should be exploited to achieve all-round education of students.

*Innovating approaches to moral and political work.* This work requires us to adapt to changing circumstances and keep in pace with the times. We must also follow the underlying principles for moral and educational work and for education in general, and bear in mind students' cognitive development. Good practices should be upheld, old ones updated, and new ones introduced to improve moral and political work comprehensively. We should shape students with culture and through social practice. We should use culture to exert gradual influence, combine education with productive labor and social practice, and help students better understand society and the country and hone their skills in social practice activities so that they can make their own contributions. Young people use the Internet so frequently that we must also go online. Whoever wins the Internet wins the youth. It is therefore highly important to make good use of new media and new technology and integrate them with traditional ways to make moral and political education more accessible, advanced, and appealing.

## 2.2 Ensuring CPC leadership over moral and political work

Moral and political work in education is important because it is critical to the overall Party leadership over education, the comprehensive implementation of the Party's education policy, and the cultivation of builders of socialism. It has far-reaching consequences as it consolidates the position of Marxism and the common ideological foundations of the Party and the people. We should therefore consider such work from the highest perspective of national political and ideological security. We must ensure that the Party guides ideology and direction of school development, and that Marxism remains the mainstream ideology of schools. In this way, we will enhance the cohesion and rallying power of socialist ideology.

---

### ❧ *Quote from Xi Jinping* ❧

While economic development is the prime task of our Party, ideological work is an extremely important task of our Party.

—Speech at the National Conference on Public Communication, August 19, 2013

---

*Ensuring the right direction for ideological work.* The education sector both produces and consumes ideas, opinions, and culture. Any ideological fault in the sector will create an enormous impact. Therefore, ideological work in education tolerates no fatal mistakes. We must ensure the correct direction, maintain constant vigilance, and never relax control. As long as the mainstream ideology is held fast and positive forces are strong, we will not be vulnerable to attacks from any direction.

*Strengthening the ideological ground.* The education sector is the forefront of our Party's values education. Different ideas and viewpoints meet and clash here. If this position is lost, we risk complete defeat. It is therefore necessary to strengthen management of positions such as classrooms and other cultural platforms. We must guard against and eliminate the erosion of schools by erroneous political thoughts and separatism. We must ensure the separation of education from religion by preventing external religious forces from infiltrating universities and guard against any religious activities on campus. We should make good use of the campus to spread core socialist values to ensure that these values soak into students' hearts and minds and guide their actions. At the same time, it is important to create innovative means of communication and make sure our Party's innovative theories are included in textbooks and classroom teaching and understood by students.

A responsibility system for ideological work should be implemented and the responsibility should be faithfully discharged. Xi Jinping pointed out that Party organization secretaries and administrative officials should assume political and leadership responsibilities. They should have the courage to step in and stand against wrongdoers. The education authorities should specify responsibilities for Party organizations at all levels and ensure the implementation of values education, the effective management of platforms, and full accountability. It is also necessary to carry out in-depth analyses of major issues in the ideological field, provide guidance on strategic tasks, and facilitate the implementation of major plans and tasks. We must be clear on matters of political principle and be ready to confront adversaries head-on. We must strengthen the supervision of school Party committees to ensure the implementation of the responsibility system. It is also necessary to improve the working mechanism by which Party committees exercise unified leadership over ideological work, and establish a mechanism in which the administrative team, trade union, and Communist Youth League all participate.

## 2.3 Fostering a team skilled in moral and political education

Overall Party leadership over education and moral work depends on talented people and teamwork. General Secretary Xi Jinping indicated that competent school officials should first and foremost exemplify moral and political work; they should use all occasions, platforms, and methods to promote moral and political education; they should involve all staff and students in this task. We should, therefore, foster a team of political personnel who can perform moral and political duties professionally in their daily activities and cater to individual needs.

*Building an adequately staffed political corps to carry out values education.* To strengthen Party institutions and improve moral education, it is essential to build a high-quality and adequately staffed team for Party affairs and political work. The creation of such a team should be included in schools' personnel management plan. It is also important to build teams of Party and administrative officials, Communist Youth League leaders, MPT teachers, philosophy and social sciences teachers, and student advisers and psychological counselors. We must ensure that these teams attract high-caliber members, attain high standards of performance, and receive a continuous supply of new personnel.

*Improving the competence of moral and political corps.* Party committees and governments at all levels and schools should manage the career path of moral and political personnel as they do for outstanding teachers and researchers. These personnel should be provided with necessary support, platforms, remuneration packages, and room for development. It is necessary to recruit candidates from wider sources, provide training opportunities, strengthen practice, and improve the incentive mechanism so that they will specialize and perform their duties more professionally.

*Strengthening the MPT teaching force.* General Secretary Xi stressed at the meeting with MPT teachers that the key to successful MPT courses lies in teachers, and that teachers need to be proactive, incentivized, and creative. MPT teachers should ignite students' desire for the true, the good, and the beautiful, and guide them to fasten their first button in life correctly.

- First, MPT teachers should be politically reliable, able to adopt the right political perspective, and sober-minded over key issues of principle. We should let those with faith preach faith.
- Second, MPT teachers should love the country, the nation, and society. They should enrich their thought by absorbing nutrients from the times, society, and the great practices of the Party and the people.

- Third, MPT teachers should be able to innovate. They should study dialectical and historical materialism, innovate classroom teaching, impress students with profound learning experiences, and help them establish correct ideals and beliefs and acquire correct perspectives.
- Fourth, MPT teachers should be visionaries. They should acquire broad knowledge, adopt historical and international perspectives, and be able to enlighten students through vivid, in-depth, and specific comparisons.
- Fifth, MPT teachers should exercise self-discipline. They should maintain consistency inside and outside classrooms, and online and offline; they should spread mainstream ideas and transmit positivity.
- Sixth, MPT teachers should be upright and charismatic. Only if a teacher is appealing to students will the latter hearken to their words. Teachers should inspire students with the strengths of their personality, win them over with the power of theory and truth, play an exemplary role, and be loved by students.

## 3. Strengthening Party Leadership in the Education System

As the saying goes, it takes a blacksmith with solid skills to forge solid tools. The CPC leadership can only be realized in education with sound organizations and solid Party work. Strengthening the Party in the education system, as an important part of the new and great project of Party advancement, enjoys a special position. Party organizations in all kinds of schools at all levels should pay attention to strengthening the Party, and regard this as a basic skill in running a school.

## 3.1 Prioritizing political work in strengthening the Party

In strengthening the Party in the new era, we should prioritize political work and see the Party's political foundations reinforced, its ideological commitment buttressed, its organizations consolidated, its conduct improved, and its discipline enforced, with institutional improvements incorporated into every aspect of these endeavors. We must step up our efforts to combat corruption. We should regard moral and political education as the basis for a strong Party presence and ensure the Party leadership in the education system.

*Putting political work at the top of the agenda in strengthening the Party.* General Secretary Xi emphasized, "Reinforcing the Party's political foundations is of fundamental importance, as it determines the direction and efficacy of the effort to strengthen the Party."[1] The purpose of the Party's political work is to strengthen political belief, political leadership, and political capacity, purify the political ecology, and realize unity of thought and action across the Party. A strong political belief requires us to equip our minds with the well-established theory of the Party, implement its political principle, and take a firm political position. Strong political leadership requires us to uphold Xi Jinping's core position in the CPC Central Committee and in the Party as a whole, and uphold the Party Central Committee's authority and its centralized, unified leadership, and improve the Party's leadership system and leadership style. A strong political capacity requires us to enhance the political functions of Party organizations, highlight the political nature of education departments, encourage mass organizations to play a political function, and improve the political competence of Party members and officials. Purifying the political ecology requires us to take the Party's political life seriously, observe its political discipline and rules, develop a positive and healthy political culture within it, emphasize the political criteria

---

1 Xi Jinping: "Secure a Decisive Victory in Building a Moderately Prosperous Society in All Respects and Strive for the Great Success of Socialism with Chinese Characteristics for a New Era," *The Governance of China*, Vol. III, Foreign Languages Press, Beijing, 2020, p. 66.

for appointment of officials, and maintain the Party's wholesome nature and integrity.

*Taking ideological work as the foundation.* Xi Jinping noted that in order to build "diamond-hard bodies" that resist corrosion, we must equip our minds with scientific theories and constantly cultivate our spiritual life. The primary task of our Party's ideological work is to strengthen our ideals and beliefs. Noble and firm beliefs will not arise spontaneously. The Party's ideological work in the education system requires us to study the fundamental tenets of Marxism, especially Xi Jinping Thought on Socialism with Chinese Characteristics for a New Era, learn to observe and solve problems from Marxist standpoints and with Marxist methods, and base our ideals and beliefs on scientific theories and correct understanding of historical laws. We should help teachers and students shape their worldview, outlook on life, and value system, maintain firm beliefs in the long-term goal of communism and the shared ideal of socialism with Chinese characteristics, faithfully put them into practice, and aspire to rejuvenate our nation.

*Advancing the Party's organization, conduct, and discipline.* The strength of our Party comes from its organizations, and its overall leadership and all its endeavors also rely on a strong organizational system. Therefore, to consolidate the Party's organizational work, it is particularly important to select and foster good leaders who are politically reliable, professionally outstanding, morally incorruptible, and well accepted by teachers and students. Party committees at all levels should be active in developing a positive work ethos. They should strengthen the foundations, address key issues, establish norms, implement responsibilities, and turn "soft indicators" into "hard constraints," so that schools are filled with vigor, vitality, and positivity and display a refreshing atmosphere of reform and innovation. Strict discipline is one of our Party's great traditions and a unique strength. The education sector should regard discipline as the fundamental approach to strict all-round governance of the Party. We should establish and tighten the Party's discipline, treat both symptoms and root causes with the discipline, and help Party members and officials fall into the habit of observing the discipline, so that we can advance the strict all-round governance of the Party in the education sector.

*Strengthening institution building throughout the Party to fight corruption.* General Secretary Xi reiterated that strict all-round governance of the Party requires us to address both ideological and institutional issues. If the Party wants to supervise its own conduct and apply strict discipline, there must be strong systems. Party organizations of the education system should implement Party rules and regulations earnestly, take intra-Party political activities seriously, develop a healthy political ecology, and constantly strengthen the Party. Party organizations should help their members and officials raise awareness of the rules, and create an atmosphere of respecting, observing, and defending them. In the fight against corruption, Party members and officials should be educated to hold discipline in awe, respect all limits, and become used to working under oversight. We need to consolidate and build on the overwhelming momentum of the anti-corruption campaign, and develop a system under which officials do not dare to be, are not able to be, and do not want to be corrupt.

*Strengthening the progressive nature and integrity to improve the rallying power and effectiveness of the Party organization in the education sector.* At a conference themed "Staying True to Our Aspiration and Founding Mission" on May 31, 2019, Xi Jinping refocused on the need to "keep to our mission, take on responsibilities, identify gaps, and ensure implementation." He noted that we must study and implement the Thought on Socialism with Chinese Characteristics for a New Era, forge loyalty, integrity, and commitment, and lead people of all ethnic groups in national rejuvenation. Through study, he said, we should become well versed in theory, morally cleansed, ready to shoulder responsibilities, and willing to solve problems for the people, and set examples as clean and just officials. His speech emphasized the significance of thematic education and put forward clear requirements for practice. The speech was important in political and ideological terms and pertinent to solving specific problems. It was a guideline for the thematic education initiative and a leading document for strengthening the Party in the new era.

The education sector should study the speech earnestly and comply with the insights expressed. We must ensure that the education initiative achieves solid results.

### 3.2 Implementing the principal-actor responsibility for strict all-round governance of the Party

The key to running China's affairs well lies in the CPC, which must implement strict discipline and self-governance. The education sector should become a stronghold upholding the Party leadership, and its Party committees should faithfully discharge their responsibilities for strict all-round governance of the Party.

Strict all-round governance of the Party requires Party committees to serve as the principal actors and discipline inspection commissions to serve as the supervisors. Party committees exercise overall leadership over schools and are fully responsible for strengthening the Party in schools. Party organizations at all levels and their persons in charge are mandate holders and must shoulder responsibility for strict governance of the Party. The commissions for discipline inspection undertake the responsibility for supervision in the governance of the Party and should strictly manage the Party in accordance with the requirements of the CPC Central Committee adopted since the 18th CPC National Congress on specialized supervision. Party organizations at all levels of the education system should concentrate on strengthening the Party, and simultaneously plan, deploy, and assess relevant work and their central tasks. The requirements that the Party supervise its own conduct and apply strict discipline should be substantively implemented.

Intra-Party political activities and purification of the political ecology within the Party should be the priorities. Party organizations should earnestly assume the duty of intra-Party supervision, and unequivocally support discipline inspection departments in doing their job. Discipline inspection departments should perform their duties as specialized supervisory organs, and regard supervision as a restraint, a caution, and an alert, so as to make the Party truly disciplined.

The Party must always abide by strict discipline and rules, and never hesitate to enforce discipline. Strict discipline has characterized Party governance since the 18th CPC National Congress. To govern the Party strictly requires uncompromising discipline. We must impose strict education, management, self-discipline, supervision, and accountability. We must improve the work ethos by checking any tendency to favor form over substance, and eliminating red tape, hedonism, and extravagance. We must be attentive to covert or indirect forms of undesirable work styles of favoring form over substance and red tape in education, in particular. We must resolutely oppose any thoughts and behaviors coveting privilege. In building a clean government, we must keep a close eye on critical positions and high-risk areas, identify management loopholes, and strive to create a healthy political ecology.

### 3.3 Strengthening grassroots Party organizations and membership

To build a house, first lay the foundations. "Grassroots Party organizations are the foundations of the Party. The building will be firm if the foundations are solid. The building will collapse if the foundations are weak."[1] We must strengthen grassroots Party organizations, lay the foundations, let grassroots Party organizations play a central role, and let Party members play an exemplary role.

*Establishing and improving Party organizations in all schools.* Xi Jinping stressed that the more complex the situation and the weaker an area's foundations, the more it is necessary to improve Party organizations and Party's services there and focus on strengthening the foundations, because a chain is only as strong as its weakest link. The education system should focus on improving organizational strength, including improving

---

1 Xi Jinping: *Speech at the National Conference on Organizational Work*, Chinese edition, People's Publishing House, 2018, p. 13.

grassroots organizations and expanding their coverage and service, optimizing the organizational setup, and streamlining hierarchical relations. We must promote all-round and solid progress in grassroots Party organizations in all schools, make such organizations the closest and most reliable ones to support teachers and students, and have them play a central role in moral education. It is necessary to improve the grassroots Party organizations in institutions of higher learning as well as primary and secondary schools, ensuring that the Party's work covers all areas. It is also necessary to bring private colleges and Chinese-foreign cooperative schools into the plan of moral education by improving our systems and mechanisms, extending our reach, establishing and improving Party organizations, and instating Party secretaries. In this way, moral and political work will cover all these schools.

*Building a contingent of high-caliber officials.* Xi Jinping emphasized that our Party and its officials are the key to winning the new struggles of the era. We must foster a team of Party officials to undertake responsibility with iron faith, iron discipline, and iron courage. Party members and officials in the education system should strictly comply with the Party Constitution and the rules for Party members—"be strict with oneself and lenient with others."[1] Party members must always behave with decorum, examine and reflect on themselves, strive to be "neither perturbed by the temptation of petty profits nor tantalized by the desires of the material world," and be honest and hardworking, clean and upright.

*Giving full play to Party members' pioneering and exemplary roles.* A Party member is a banner. By setting an example, Party members encourage other people to follow. We should thus strengthen the education of Party members, and encourage them to hold themselves to higher standards, take the lead, do solid work, and act as role models. Party members should not be shy of presenting their Party identity and establishing

---

1 Cited from *The Book of History*, a collection of documents and speeches by rulers of the Shang (*c.* 1600-1046 BC) and Zhou (1046-256 BC) dynasties.

high standards. Teacher and student Party members should strengthen their Party consciousness and rally fellow teachers and students. As Party members, they should be loyal to the Party, follow the Party's guidelines, work for the Party, and be vanguards and role models.

# Chapter 2

## Cultivation of New Generations of Talent with Strong Moral Character

Fostering strong moral character through education is of vital importance for the continuously thriving cause of the CPC and for the future of China. General Secretary Xi Jinping emphasizes that building moral character is a fundamental task of socialist education. Schools should be committed to the mission of cultivating talent for the Party and the state, and make the formation of morals the core of their work. Schools should advocate and practice the core socialist values, cultivate a new generation capable of shouldering the mission of national rejuvenation, and foster new generations for the socialist cause—generations with strong moral, intellectual, physical, and aesthetic grounding and with a love for labor.

# 1. Education for Building Strong Moral Character

Xi Jinping has paid great attention to the cultivation of strong moral character in education. Since the 18th CPC National Congress held in 2012, he has emphasized on several occasions the importance of moral education in nurturing new generations of socialist builders who are morally, intellectually, physically, and aesthetically developed with a love for labor. On this issue of fundamental importance, we must take an unambiguous stand.

## 1.1 Morality as the basis for national prosperity and personal success

"Virtue is the root."[1] It is the foundation for both individuals and society, and the ultimate force of progress of a country, a nation, and society. Since the 18th CPC National Congress, Xi Jinping has advised teachers and students to "know great virtues, maintain public virtues, and practice personal virtues." At the meeting with teachers and students of Peking University in May 2014, he noted that the greatest virtue is to serve the country and the people. Only with great virtues can a person realize a great cause. In the meantime, one needs to cultivate public and personal virtues. "Learn from the best that may appear and correct any mistakes that may occur."[2] We need to start to

---

1 Cited from *The Great Learning*. The original sentence reads, "Virtue is the root, and wealth is the end."
2 Cited from *The Book of Changes*, a Chinese classic of the pre-Qin period (before 221 BC) that expounds the changes of everything in the world. It is said to be the theoretical root of natural philosophy in traditional Chinese thinking.

do small things well and be self-disciplined even in trivial matters.

A prosperous and strong country and national rejuvenation require spiritual and moral support. Xi Jinping noted, "To realize the Chinese Dream of national rejuvenation, we must be wealthy in both material and cultural terms..."[1] As a precious spiritual asset, virtue plays an important role in regulating conduct, maintaining social order, and building healthy social ethos. As long as society strives to cultivate morality and promote virtuous conduct, and as long as the Chinese nation observes high moral standards, we will be able to gather strong spiritual and moral support for the Chinese Dream, and our nation will be healthy, enterprising, and full of hope.

For a human being, the most important thing is to cultivate morality. Moral integrity is the prerequisite for a successful career and academic life. It is the foundation of a person's life. Without a noble mind and a strong moral character, young people will not become outstanding even if they are erudite. In the early days of his tenure as secretary of the CPC Zhejiang Provincial Committee, Xi Jinping noted, "A person without virtue will not go far. Without moral integrity, no one will be able to accomplish great things even if they have profound learning."[2] Talent assists morality; morality commands talent. Traditional Chinese culture pays special attention to morals, placing talent in a secondary position. Without morals, it will be difficult for one to become a useful person, let alone a master of any trade. This explains why we select those with both morals and talent for our work, with morality as a priority, because virtue is primary and provides direction. One is suitable for an official position only if he or she knows great virtues, maintains public virtues, and practices personal virtues.

---

1 Xi Jinping: *The Governance of China*, Vol. II, Foreign Languages Press, Beijing, 2017, p. 352.
2 Xi Jinping: *Down to Earth and at the Forefront—Thoughts and Actions on Promoting the Development of Zhejiang*, Chinese edition, Central Party School Press, Beijing, 2006, p. 304.

## 1.2 Cultivating virtues as the fundamental task of schools

> ～◈〜*Quote from Xi Jinping*〜◈～
>
> Education is a process of cultivating virtue and competence. People without virtue cannot establish themselves. Cultivating morals should therefore be taken as the central task of education. This is the dialectics of education.
>
> —Speech at the meeting with teachers and students of Peking University, May 2, 2018

Schools are the primary venue for education. Although economic and social development requires schools to assume other responsibilities, education remains their most fundamental charge. Education is necessarily an integrated process of cultivating virtue and competence, with the former being at the root. The foundation of education lies in building strong moral character. To turn young people into outstanding talent, schools must effectively impart knowledge, and more importantly, engage in moral education. In September 2016, during a visit to his alma mater Beijing Bayi School, Xi Jinping pointed out that basic education is a cause for building moral character. He said that the teaching of correct thinking, ethics, and core socialist values should be reinforced in order to help students develop a strong sense of self-esteem, self-confidence, self-reliance, and self-improvement. In December of the same year, he once again emphasized, at the National Conference on Moral and Political Work in Institutions of Higher Learning, that establishing virtues is the fundamental task of universities.

All schools must make moral education their fundamental task and integrate it into all aspects of education management. We must make sure that building strong moral character sits at the root of personnel training. In September 2018, General Secretary Xi noted at the National Education Conference that moral education should be incorporated in ideological and ethical courses, knowledge acquisition, and social practices; it should run through basic education, technical and vocational education, and higher education. Practices that run counter to moral education should be resolutely corrected. Efforts should be made to establish dynamic, productive, and inclusive institutions and mechanisms, enabling schools to cultivate morals.

### 1.3 Moral criterion: key to assessing all education initiatives

In May 2018, Xi Jinping emphasized at the meeting with teachers and students of Peking University that the outcome of moral education should be taken as the fundamental criterion for appraising all school work. Schools should set up an education system in which morals take priority and students are cultivated with sound values and ethics.

This fundamental criterion should be implemented through specific elements, such as education models, school operations, management, and logistics. These systems should be adapted into long-term mechanisms that promote the physical and mental health and all-round development of students. Schools should improve the evaluation of students so that teachers may cultivate morality. Criteria that only consider test scores, admission rates, academic degrees, number of publications, and professional and technical titles should be abandoned. Schools should be able to balance the vigor of management with the subtle approaches necessary for moral education. Elements suitable for moral education in courses should be exploited and the moral and political theory courses should be improved. Schools, families, and society should form an organic whole in moral education. The Party and government departments, social organizations, businesses, and public service institutions, as well as sub-districts and community organizations should all play a part in moral education.

## 2. Incorporating Core Socialist Values into the National Education System

The core socialist values are essentially virtues—virtues for individuals and for the state and society at large. They are the foundation of the state and the soul of the nation. Since the 18th CPC National Congress, General Secretary Xi has made systematic, rich, and insightful statements on cultivating and practicing core socialist values, and has issued clear requirements for fostering a new generation capable of shouldering the mission of national rejuvenation.

## 2.1 Core socialist values: the spirit of contemporary China

To realize the Chinese Dream, we should carry forward the Chinese spirit, a spirit that can be defined as the national spirit with patriotism at its core, and a spirit of the times with reform and innovation at its core. Xi Jinping noted, "The core socialist values represent the contemporary Chinese spirit and are a crystallization of the values shared by all Chinese people."[1] The values of prosperity, democracy, civility, and harmony are meant for the country; freedom, equality, justice, and the rule of law are meant for society; and patriotism, dedication, integrity, and friendliness are meant for citizens. The core socialist values combine all of the above. They explain what sort of country and society we are striving for, and what kind of citizens we are cultivating.

Cultivating and disseminating the core socialist values is a social project to foster national cohesion and reinforce our foundations. Xi Jinping noted that the core values carry the spiritual aspiration of a nation and country, and represent the standards for judging right and wrong. He said, "Without shared core values, a nation and country will be at a loss to know what is right and what is wrong, and its people will have no code of conduct to follow, the result being that the nation and country can never progress."[2] In essence, soft power depends on the vitality, cohesion, and appeal of the core values of a nation. Therefore,

---

1 Xi Jinping: "Secure a Decisive Victory in Building a Moderately Prosperous Society in All Respects and Strive for the Great Success of Socialism with Chinese Characteristics for a New Era," *The Governance of China*, Vol. III, Foreign Languages Press, Beijing, 2020, p. 45.
2 Xi Jinping: *Young People Should Practice the Core Socialist Values—Speech at the Meeting with Teachers and Students of Peking University*, Chinese edition, People's Publishing House, Beijing, 2014, p. 4.

cultivating and disseminating the core values and effectively integrating social consciousness is an important means of ensuring that the social system operates in a normal manner and that the social order is effectively maintained. It is also a major aspect of the state governance system and capacity.

## 2.2 The fundamental role of education in cultivating and practicing core socialist values

Education is the basic tool to cultivate core socialist values. It shapes souls, lives, and people. All types of education cultivate values. Incorporating core socialist values into the entire process and every aspect of education represents the intrinsic requirement of socialist education, because it addresses the fundamental questions of what talent to foster, how, and for whom. In 2017, Xi Jinping noted in his report to the 19th CPC National Congress, "We will focus on fostering a new generation capable of shouldering the mission of national rejuvenation; we will offer them better guidance, expose them to practice, and provide institutional guarantees. We will draw on the core socialist values to guide education, efforts to raise cultural-ethical standards, and the creation, production, and distribution of cultural and intellectual products, and see that all areas of social development are imbued with these values and that they become part of people's thinking and behavior."[1]

Fostering core socialist values must start with children. Schools must ensure that the values are included in textbooks and classroom teaching and understood by students. We must be persistent in disseminating Marxist theory and core socialist values and do so by incorporating them into the whole process of education—from basic to higher education, and from general to technical and vocational education. We must prioritize morals and core socialist values in all schools, for all

---

1 Xi Jinping: "Secure a Decisive Victory in Building a Moderately Prosperous Society in All Respects and Strive for the Great Success of Socialism with Chinese Characteristics for a New Era," *The Governance of China*, Vol. III, Foreign Languages Press, Beijing, 2020, p. 45.

students, in all aspects of teaching, and in management, thus forming a multi-dimensional education model consisting of classroom teaching, social practice, campus culture, and online education.

We must enhance morals and ethics in children and college students in line with their stages of development as well as their mental and physical characteristics. Guided by the core socialist values, efforts should be made to develop moral education curricula and textbooks connecting primary, secondary, and higher education. We need to improve the network where schools, families, and society work together for a common goal. Families and society are encouraged to collaborate with schools to consolidate educational outcomes by creating a positive family and social ethos. The three actors working together will create a strong synergy.

## 2.3 Helping younger generations "fasten the first button of life correctly"

Since antiquity, it has always been from youth that heroes have emerged. When leading the whole nation toward the Two Centenary Goals and national rejuvenation, General Secretary Xi has paid special attention to the healthy growth of young people and is full of hope for their future. Looking into the future, he refers to young people as the "Dream Team" for national rejuvenation. He urges them to act now, starting from small things and with themselves. He says that young people should follow the core socialist values in their life and studies, and do their best to disseminate the values in society; they should put their youthful dreams into action in the course of realizing the Chinese Dream of national rejuvenation and their personal values.

*Quote from Xi Jinping*

A country will be full of hope and have a great tomorrow only when its younger generations have ideals, ability, and a strong sense of responsibility.

—Report to the 19th CPC National Congress, October 18, 2017

A nation will prosper only when its youth thrive; a country will be powerful only when its youth are strong. In his report to the 19th CPC National Congress, Xi Jinping pointed out, "The Chinese Dream is a dream about the past, the present, and the future. It is a dream of our generation, but even more so, a dream of the younger generations. The Chinese Dream of national rejuvenation will be realized ultimately through the endeavors of young people, generation by generation."[1] At the meeting with teachers and students of Peking University in May 2014, he expounded the importance of cultivating the core socialist values in young people by drawing on the analogy of "fastening the first button of life correctly." He said, "Why am I talking about the core socialist values with you young people? Because your value orientation will decide the values of the whole of society in the years to come. Besides, young people are at the time of life when they form and establish their values. It is therefore very important to offer some guidance. That reminds me of something that happens in our daily life. When we button up our coat, we may inadvertently put the first button in the wrong button hole, and that will result in all the other buttons being put in the wrong holes. That's why we say that young people should 'button right' in the early days of their life."[2] He urged young people to study diligently, acquire true knowledge, foster virtue, behave ethically, discern right from wrong, make correct decisions, be honest, sincere and upright, and do solid work.

If children are wise, the country will be wise; if children are strong, the country will be strong. Xi Jinping has paid great attention to the growth of children and spoken vividly on the importance of cultivating core socialist values among them. He has said on several occasions that every adult grows up from a child; the future is always created by today's

---

1 Xi Jinping: "Secure a Decisive Victory in Building a Moderately Prosperous Society in All Respects and Strive for the Great Success of Socialism with Chinese Characteristics for a New Era," *The Governance of China*, Vol. III, Foreign Languages Press, Beijing, 2020, p. 75.
2 Xi Jinping: *The Governance of China*, Vol. I, Foreign Languages Press, Beijing, 2018, pp. 191-192.

children; children are the future of our country and the hope of the Chinese nation. In May 2014, in his speech at a meeting held at Minzu Primary School of Haidian District in Beijing, he said, "To create a better future for our nation we need to encourage our children to set great goals and shape their characters, and ensure a sound environment for their growth."[1] In May 2018, in his reply to a letter from Beiliang Red Army Primary School in Zhaojin of Shaanxi province, Xi Jinping expressed his hope that the students should study the history of Chinese revolution, development, and reform, follow the example of heroes and role models, love the Party, the country and the people, and pass on the fine revolutionary traditions.

Fostering core socialist values among children must be done in a way that conforms to their age and traits. For this, General Secretary Xi has raised four points: remembering the requirements, following role models, starting from childhood, and accepting advice. Remembering the requirements means that children need to learn by heart the core socialist values and always keep these values in mind. They will gradually gain a better understanding of them as they grow up and acquire more knowledge and experience. Following role models means that children need to learn from heroes and model figures and to cultivate character through emulation. Starting from childhood means that children need to start with themselves, and make every possible effort to cultivate good morals. Accepting advice means that children should be ready to accept both suggestions and criticisms, and grow up in a good environment where they correct their mistakes and become better persons. Children should form the habit of strict self-discipline early on in life and always be ready to accept advice.

---

1 Xi Jinping: *The Governance of China*, Vol. I, Foreign Languages Press, Beijing, 2018, pp. 201-202.

## 2.4 Teachers and students as firm believers, active communicators, and model practitioners of core socialist values

In the course of cultivating and promoting the core socialist values, Xi Jinping attaches great importance to the initiative and creativity of teachers and students. At the meeting with teachers and students of Peking University in May 2014, he urged them to uphold the core socialist values and build a successful career by serving the nation. In his speech at the National Conference on Moral and Political Work in Institutions of Higher Learning in 2016, he clearly stated, "We should promote and practice the core socialist values, and guide teachers and students to be firm believers, active communicators, and model practitioners of these values."[1]

Teachers should set good examples in promoting and practicing core socialist values. In 2014, at the meeting with teachers and students of Beijing Normal University, Xi Jinping noted, "Teachers should make the best use of the classroom, the campus, and their own actions to promote core socialist values; they should use their knowledge and experience to ignite students' aspirations for the true, the good, and the beautiful so that these values can be infused into students' hearts and minds and transformed into their daily behavior, thus enhancing their ability to choose and apply the right values in the process of growing up."[2] He noted that teachers bear the important responsibility of nurturing the next generation; their ideals, faith, and values are light beacons illuminating the students' path. Teachers should always stand together with the Party and the people, be loyal followers and practitioners of Chinese socialism, implement the CPC's education policy in the entire education process, and treat this work seriously. In 2016, he further remarked

---

1 Xi Jinping: *The Governance of China*, Vol. II, Foreign Languages Press, Beijing, 2017, p. 407.
2 Xi Jinping: *Being a Good Teacher to the Satisfaction of the Communist Party of China and the People—Speech at the Meeting with Teachers and Students of Beijing Normal University*, Chinese edition, People's Publishing House, Beijing, 2014, p. 6.

at the National Conference on Moral and Political Work in Institutions of Higher Learning that teachers are the engineers of the human soul, who undertake the essential mission of shaping the mind. Teachers must have a thorough understanding of and a firm faith in what they teach. They should first receive an education themselves. He asked teachers to become a mirror for students, disseminators of advanced ideas and culture, strong supporters of CPC leadership, and mentors who can win students' respect with their charisma and lead the students by setting good examples.

## 2.5 Creating an environment conducive to cultivating and practicing core socialist values

Xi Jinping has emphasized that to cultivate and practice core socialist values and help the younger generations "fasten the first button in life correctly" is a long-term, systematic endeavor that cannot be accomplished at one stroke; nor can it rely solely on the strength of schools. Rather, it requires the concerted efforts of the whole society.

We should lead social ethos by example. The power of example is enormous. Xi Jinping has called on all Party members and officials to take the lead in studying and spreading the core socialist values, to influence other people by their exemplary behavior and moral character, and to set a good example for the youth. Departments concerned with public communication should make exemplary acts better known and create an environment where heroes are respected, admired, and emulated.

Young people should learn from heroes, advanced figures, and models from all walks of life, taking them as role models. He has urged writers and artists to put people first in their works, develop a sound understanding of China's history, national viewpoint, state outlook, and cultural perspectives, and extol those who work hard for the interests of the people; he has also urged them to tell China's stories well, communicate the Chinese spirit, showcase the Chinese achievements, and reject vulgarity and kitsch in literary and artistic creation. He has said that cultural workers should help refine people's tastes and develop uplifting interests through their own integrity and healthy literary and artistic works, enlighten people's minds, and foster a positive social ethos so as to provide the younger generations with colorful and healthy spiritual food.

Core socialist values should be integrated into the rule of law and social systems. The values are the soul of our socialist legal system. Integrating core socialist values into law-based governance is an essential requirement for combining the rule of law with the rule by virtue, and an important way to strengthen the core socialist values. Xi Jinping emphasizes that we must uphold the core socialist values when strengthening rules and regulations in all sectors, and when formulating codes of conduct for students and residential communities, and turn these values into basic guidance for people's daily life and work. We should create ceremonies and conduct various memorial and celebration events to disseminate mainstream values and enhance people's sense of identity and belonging. Efforts should be made to integrate the requirements of the core socialist values into various activities concerning intellectual and cultural progress and attract people to participate in such activities.

Family values, family education, and family bonds play an irreplaceable role in the cultivation and practice of core socialist values. General Secretary Xi himself was deeply influenced by his family culture. His father, Xi Zhongxun, was strict with his children. He never allowed his official vehicle to be used for private purposes. He placed his children at boarding schools and asked them to return home by bus on weekends. Xi Jinping has inherited his father's character of strict self-discipline, frugality, and honesty. In the early 1980s, when Xi Jinping was dispatched from Beijing to Zhengding county, Hebei province to serve as deputy secretary of the county's Party committee, all he brought with him was an old army quilt and a patched cotton mattress. In a letter of congratulations on his father's birthday, Xi Jinping wrote, "Father's thriftiness borders on self-denial. The strictness of our family education is also well known. We all developed the habit of thrift from Father's education."[1] At the gathering to celebrate the Spring Festival of 2015, Xi Jinping noted that family is the cell of society and the first school of life. No matter how times change or how life changes, family values, family education, and family bonds must be emphasized. Parents should teach their children with their own words and deeds, giving them both knowledge and virtue and practicing what they teach. They should help their children "fasten the first button in life correctly" and take the first step on the ladder of life correctly.

A good online environment is crucial to the cultivation and practice of core socialist values. Xi Jinping has noted that cyberspace is a shared virtual home for hundreds of millions of people. A clean and sound online environment is in the best interests of the people, while a foul and volatile one is not. The Internet is not a lawless place: the use of the Internet to advocate, incite, and preach the toppling of the government, religious extremism, and separatism must be resolutely opposed and stopped; the use of the Internet to engage in fraud, circulate obscene materials, or make personal attacks must also be prohibited. Meanwhile, positive information should be provided on the Internet to foster a sound and uplifting cyber culture. We need to nurture people's hearts and nourish society with the core socialist values as well as the fine achievements of human civilization, ensuring that positive energy and mainstream values prevail. By doing so, we will be able to create a clean and sound cyberspace for Internet users, especially the young.

## 3. Nurturing New Generations of Socialist Builders with Well-Rounded Development

The Marxist idea of people's all-round development is the theoretical

---

1 Editorial Board: *The Biography of Xi Zhongxun,* Vol. II, Chinese edition, Central Party Literature Press, Beijing, 2013, p. 643.

basis of China's education policy. At the National Education Conference, General Secretary Xi, speaking from the strategic perspective of the overall development of the Party and the state, articulated the fundamental goal of education as nurturing a new generation of capable young people who are morally, intellectually, physically, and aesthetically developed with a love for labor and are well-prepared to join the socialist cause, and clarified the six key tasks of cultivating new generations for the socialist cause, providing fundamental guidelines for fostering virtue through education.

## 3.1 Cultivating new generations of socialist builders as the fundamental objective of education

The fundamental question of education is what kind of people to train. "When the virtuous are numerous in the state, order will be stable; when the virtuous are few, order will be unstable."[1] From ancient to modern times, all countries have cultivated people according to their own political requirements. The People's Republic of China is a socialist country led by the Communist Party of China, which determines that the fundamental task of our education must be nurturing new builders of socialism, or talent who support the leadership of the CPC and the country's socialist system and devote their lives to China's socialist cause. This is the ultimate goal of our education and modern education system. In 2018, General Secretary Xi emphasized at the meeting with teachers and students of Peking University, "Cultivating the people needed for social development is, to be specific, to train those required for social development, knowledge accumulation, cultural inheritance, national survival, and system functioning."[2] "Socialist" is the very defining word for new generations of socialist builders, because it determines the

---

1 Cited from *Mozi*, a philosophical work written by Mozi (*c.* 468-376 BC) and his disciples in the Warring States Period (475-221 BC).
2 Xi Jinping: *Speech at the Meeting with Teachers and Students of Peking University*, Chinese edition, People's Publishing House, Beijing, 2018, p. 5.

fundamental task of education. No matter what era it is, education must always serve the mission of nurturing people for the Party and the country.

What essential qualities and mindset should future builders of socialism possess? Xi Jinping has noted that they should have moral integrity as well as solid skills and knowledge. The new era and new conditions have set out new and higher requirements for such people, including moral integrity, knowledge, innovative skills, and practical capabilities, as well as physical health, artistic ability, humanistic quality, and employment skills. The people we cultivate must uphold the long-term goal of communism and the shared ideal of socialism with Chinese characteristics; they must be patriotic and never forget their national identity; they must constantly improve themselves through moral development; they must be knowledgeable and possess a global vision; they must have lofty goals and a courageous spirit of striving forward; and they must be morally, intellectually, physically, and aesthetically developed with a love for labor.

### 3.2 Endeavoring to train new generations of socialist builders

The competence of youth directly bears on the pace of realizing the Chinese Dream. How, then, should future builders of socialism be fostered? General Secretary Xi has highlighted the following six respects.

First, we should foster firm beliefs. At the National Conference on Public Communication in 2018, Xi Jinping pointed out that the top priority in fostering a new generation capable of shouldering the mission of national rejuvenation is to build firm ideals and beliefs among students. Students should be taught the long-term goal of communism and the shared ideal of socialism with Chinese characteristics. The history of a nation is its foundation. Schools at all levels should strengthen education on Chinese history, especially modern Chinese history, the history of Chinese revolution, the Communist Party of China, the People's Republic of China, and China's reform and opening up, so that students will realize that only socialism can preserve China and only socialism with Chinese characteristics can bring development opportunities to China and lead us to national rejuvenation. Incoming builders of socialism in the new era should conscientiously develop the ideals and faith required by our times and aspire to shoulder the responsibility of national rejuvenation.

---

### ⊗ Quote from Xi Jinping ⊗

Ideals provide direction in life, and convictions determine the success of a cause. Without ideals and convictions, one suffers from spiritual malnutrition.

—Speech at the meeting with young representatives from all walks of life, May 4, 2013

---

Second, we should foster patriotism. Love of one's country is the most lasting and profound emotion of humanity, and the foundation of virtue and achievements. It is the core of the ethos of the Chinese nation. To promote patriotism, we must start with children, incorporate patriotism into the whole process of cultural and ethical education, help students develop a sound understanding of history, nation, state, and culture, enhance patriotic awareness, strengthen national pride and cultural self-confidence, and firm up the patriotic spirit in their hearts. The future of the motherland is inextricably linked with the future of the Party and socialism. Xi Jinping has repeatedly emphasized that only by loving the country, the Party, and socialism can patriotism be refreshing and real. It is the most important manifestation of patriotism in contemporary China. Young people should align their ideals and actions with the future of their motherland and the nation, support the Communist Party of China, uphold the Party leadership, take a people-centered approach, and dedicate their lives to the country.

Third, we should foster virtue. We must help students nurture and practice core socialist values, improve integrity, and become citizens with great love, virtue, and noble ideals. When talking about cultivating morality, one needs to have high ambitions as well as pragmatic plans.

One needs to learn to work, to be thrifty, to be grateful, to be helpful, to be modest, to be tolerant, to examine oneself, and to exercise self-restraint. To strengthen morality, we should draw nutrition from traditional Chinese culture. We must creatively transform and develop Chinese traditions, so that the cultural artifacts displayed at museums and heritage sites around the country and the teachings from ancient books can all come to life and be passed down from generation to generation. Law ensures social stability while virtue nourishes the mind. Law is a set of virtues in writing, whereas virtue represents the law in one's inner world. It is necessary to strengthen students' awareness of the need to uphold the rule of law, so that they can develop the habits of abiding by the law.

Fourth, we should increase students' knowledge and experience. An ancient Chinese saying goes, "Study, like a crossbow, is the source of power; talent, like a sharp arrowhead, can hit its goal only when guided by knowledge and experience."[1] Studying is the ladder for progress, while practice is the way to hone skills and gain insight. Young people are in the prime time of learning. Xi Jinping has urged them to take learning as the first priority, a responsibility, a moral endeavor, and a lifestyle, and establish a conviction that dreams start from study and career success depends on competence. He has said that young people should make diligence a driving force of their youthful journey and competence a strength in their youthful endeavors. Young people should treasure their time, seek knowledge without distractions, broaden their vision, and enrich their minds; they should work hard to seek truth, explore reason, and make wise judgments. The 19th CPC National Congress concluded that the new era will be a period in which China will move closer to the global center stage and make a greater contribution to humanity. As the incoming builders of socialism in the new era, the young should not only love their motherland, but also acquire a global vision and competence to

---

1 Cited from *Sequel to Discourses on Poetry* by Yuan Mei (1716-1798), a poet in the Qing dynasty (1616-1911).

serve not only China, but also the world and the whole humanity.

Fifth, we should foster students' unyielding spirit. The majority of today's young people have grown up in an environment where they do not need to worry about food and clothing. Therefore, they especially need to develop a sense of responsibility, strong will, and the spirit of hard work. In 2018, at the meeting with teachers and students of Peking University, General Secretary Xi expressed his wish that university students should "set high ambitions and become trailblazers." "Those who made great achievements in ancient times had not only exceptional talent but also a strong will."[1] "If the will is not established, nothing can be accomplished in the world."[2] This needs to be buttressed with practical efforts. Empty words harm the country, while hard work makes it flourish. Socialism is to be built through hard work, so is the new era. Our country and our nation have stepped out of poverty and weakness thanks to the tenacity and hard work of generations and a spirit of constant self-improvement. "Do not set easy goals and never dodge difficulties."[3] We need to educate our students on their mission, their sense of responsibility, and their unyielding spirit, and foster their courage and optimism. Young people should seek knowledge through practice, guide their practice with knowledge, and integrate knowledge and practice. They should be persevering and ambitious, and ceaselessly improve themselves.

Sixth, we should ensure the all-round development of students. Future builders of socialism should be morally, intellectually, physically, and aesthetically developed with a love for labor. Schools should foster their comprehensive abilities: innovative thinking, curiosity, and imagination. Innovation should be carried out in all educational activities. Students should be encouraged to generate new ideas and practice anywhere and

---

1 Cited from "On Chao Cuo the Reformist" by Su Shi (1037-1101) of the Northern Song dynasty (960-1127).
2 Cited from "Longchang Academy Rules" by Wang Yangming (1472-1529) of the Ming dynasty (1368-1644).
3 Fan Ye (398-445): *The Book of the Later Han*, Chinese edition, Zhonghua Book Company, 2005, p. 1260.

at any time. Through a creative education system, we can cultivate creative talent who will make China an innovative nation.

Health is the prerequisite for all-round human development. The healthy growth of young people is critical to the future of the nation and is the greatest wish of every family. In recent years, the physical growth of China's youth has seen continuous improvement. At the same time, however, obesity and myopia among young Chinese continue to rise. In response to the high incidence of myopia and occurrence at younger ages, Xi Jinping has noted that this is a major problem with implications for the future of the country and the nation, and should be given close attention and must be stopped. Educational institutions at all levels should establish a "health first" concept, and make students aware that they assume the first responsibility for their own health. In the meantime, schools should offer a robust physical education program, so that students can enjoy their time, build their body, improve their character, and strengthen their will.

Aesthetic education is an important stepping stone to a wholesome character and spiritual enrichment. A life without the nourishment of beauty is bound to be boring and dull. It is impossible for young people to achieve all-round development if fairy tales and ballads, beautiful clouds and flowers, singing birds and insects, musical notes and rich colors, and classes of arts and crafts are absent from their lives. In August 2018, when he replied to a letter from eight senior professors from the Central Academy of Fine Arts in Beijing, General Secretary Xi emphasized the importance of aesthetic education. He noted that high moral standards must be applied in aesthetic education, calling on educators to stay rooted in real life, abide by the laws of aesthetics, carry forward the Chinese spirit of aesthetic education, and ensure both the physical and mental health of the next generation. We should strengthen and improve aesthetic and humanities education in schools and cultivate the aesthetic taste of students.

We must promote the value of work among students. Labor separates humans from animals. Labor and creativity have been important drivers of human progress. As a Chinese saying goes, "Poverty is a stranger to industry."[1] The Chinese are known as a hardworking and inventive people. Labor can foster virtue, increase wisdom, strengthen the body, and nurture aesthetic taste. General Secretary Xi has observed on many occasions the value of labor in his growth. During his stay in the small village of Liangjiahe in Shaanxi province (1969–1975), he stood together with the villagers through thick and thin, always took the initiative to do all types of difficult, dirty, and dangerous work, and never slacked off. Looking back at this experience, he has said, "Those seven years of hardship offered a great life experience to me. After that, whenever I came across difficulties, I would think of my time at Liangjiahe. If we could accomplish something even in those circumstances, then nothing is impossible, because life could not get any harsher than that." "When you encounter difficulties, you think of this experience, and you will feel there is no problem that cannot be resolved."[2] This hard experience has forged his strong will and the spirit of struggle, and his emotional attachment to the people.

At present, there are certain problems in our labor education, as young students today have fewer opportunities to do manual work and lack an understanding of labor. Some students do not know how to work; they look down upon labor and do not treasure the fruits of labor. This is not conducive to their healthy growth. The whole society should promote the value of work, and educate students to honor and respect labor, so that they can support themselves with diligent, honest, and creative work when they grow up. We need to foster a social environment that treats labor as the most glorious, noble, and beautiful.

---

1 Zuo Qiuming: *Zuo's Commentary on the Spring and Autumn Annals*, Chinese edition, Zhonghua Book Company, 1987, p. 417.
2 Central Party School Editorial Office for Official Collection of Interviews: *Xi Jinping's Seven Years as an Educated Youth*, Chinese edition, Central Party School Press, Beijing, 2017, p. 442.

### 3.3 Realizing the aspirations of our youth in the course of realizing the Chinese Dream

The Chinese Dream is the dream of our country, our nation, and every Chinese, including our youth. Every generation of young people has their own opportunities and they need to plan their life and make history under the specific circumstances that apply. Xi Jinping remarked at a ceremony to mark the centenary of the May Fourth Movement, "Our youth are the most active and vibrant force in society; they are the hope of the country and the future of the nation. Today, the youth of China are in the best time of our nation, which provides rare opportunities for career development and service to the nation."[1] As a Chinese saying goes, "The finer details fall into place when they align with the broader picture."[2] Only by integrating personal goals with the cause of the nation can young people ultimately achieve success. They should cherish their youth, have ambitions, answer the call of the times, and contribute their talents and strength to realizing the Chinese Dream.

Young people are the most energetic and are full of dreams. In modern times, the dreams of the youth in China have been closely associated with the historical process of national rejuvenation. During the

───────────────

1 Xi Jinping: *Speech at the Ceremony to Mark the Centenary of the May Fourth Movement*, Chinese edition, People's Publishing House, Beijing, 2019, p. 6.
2 Cited from "Three Questions About *The Book of Changes*" by Ouyang Xiu (1007-1072), a literary giant in the Northern Song dynasty (960-1127).

revolutionary wartime, the Chinese youth fought for national independence and peoples' liberation and many sacrificed their lives. In the early years of the People's Republic of China when the country was engaged in socialist revolution and economic development, young people responded to the CPC's call to defend our homes and toil in remote or rural areas and under harsh circumstances. In the era of reform and opening up, our youth sounded the call for united efforts to revitalize the Chinese nation and acted with one mind to build a strong and prosperous country. Looking ahead, we can see that China's younger generations have a promising future, and will accomplish much. It is a law of history that "the waves of the Yangtze River from behind drive on those ahead," and it is the responsibility of young people to surpass the achievements of their elders. During the periods of revolution, economic development, and reform, our Party has always valued, cared about, and trusted young people, and placed great expectations on the younger generations. The Party believes that young people represent the future of our country and the hope of our nation, regards them as a vital force for the cause of the Party and the people, and always encourages them to realize their ideals while serving the great cause of the people.

Future builders of socialism must dare to innovate and create. Young people are the most dynamic and most creative group of our society, and should stand in the forefront of innovation and creation. General Secretary Xi has called upon young people to dare to be the first, boldly free their minds and progress with the times, dare to seek high and low for a way to forge ahead, and be ambitious to learn from older generations and then surpass their achievements. With their youthful energy, young people can create a country and a nation full of vitality. Young people should have the willpower to cut paths through mountains and build bridges over rivers, and be indomitable and advance bravely in bringing forth new ideas. They should have a pragmatic attitude and pursue truth, and accumulate experience and achieve results through constant innovation in their own work. Happiness is not a free lunch. Nor is it a shower of rain falling from the sky. All achievements and happiness in this world come from labor and creative work. Times and life conditions are changing. Young people should equip themselves with new ideas, knowledge, and skills to adapt to the new era and create a new life.

If future builders of socialism are to make a difference, they must join in the great cause of national rejuvenation. Every generation has its own mission and responsibilities. At the meeting with teachers and students of Peking University in 2014, Xi Jinping noted, "Today, the majority of college students are around the age of 20; and they will be under the age of 30 by 2020, when we complete the building of a moderately prosperous society in all respects. They will be around 60 by the mid-21st century, when we basically realize our country's modernization. That is to say, you will participate in the cause of reaching the Two Centenary Goals along with myriads of other young people. I believe that life is meaningless for anyone without faith, without dreams, without concerted endeavors, and without contributions. I hope that you can create your own wonderful life while making the Chinese Dream come true since you have never been given a platform as spacious as this or as promising as this."[1]

Today's young people were born at the right time, but they also have a heavy responsibility. Our country is becoming prosperous and strong; our nation is marching toward rejuvenation; our people are enjoying a happier and better life. The worthy way to spend one's youth is to work with the people, advance with the people, and share the dreams of the people. As future builders of socialism, young people should uphold ideals and faith, aim high, be pragmatic, and ride on the waves of the times. They should put their youthful dreams into action in the course of national rejuvenation, and write a brilliant chapter for themselves in the tireless efforts for the benefit of the people.

---

1 Xi Jinping: *The Governance of China*, Vol. I, Foreign Languages Press, Beijing, 2018, p. 196.

# Chapter 3

## Education: a Priority for the Party and the State

A country thrives when it has a well-developed education system. Since the 18th CPC National Congress, the CPC Central Committee with Xi Jinping at the core has attached great importance to education and made major plans to prioritize and modernize education, and build an educational powerhouse. General Secretary Xi has noted that education affects the development of the country and the future of the nation and will benefit generations to come. It is, therefore, of great significance to give full play to the fundamental, guiding, and all-encompassing role of education.

# 1. The Decisive Role of Education in the Present and the Future of Humanity

Education is a fundamental way for humanity to pass on culture and knowledge, raise new generations, and create a better life for all. It is through education that humanity can train talent for society, impart and update what is known, and explore what remains to be discovered. This way, we can better understand and change the world, and create a better future for humanity.

## 1.1 Education: an important means for people's well-rounded development

An individual's character underpins his or her secular existence, and skills are essential for engaging in a professional career. General Secretary Xi has emphasized, "The quality of the workforce is vital to the development of a country and a nation. The more knowledge and talent the workforce possesses, the more creativity they will be able to unleash."[1] Against a background of ever intense international competition, whether a country can get a head start in its development increasingly depends on the character of its people, and especially the caliber of its workforce. Improving the overall quality of the workforce, as well as the entire nation, is a long-term strategy that affects national development.

As an endeavor for cultivating talent, education plays an important

---

1 Xi Jinping: *Speech at the Celebration of the International Labor Day and the Conference of Commending National Model Workers and Advanced Workers*, Chinese edition, People's Publishing House, Beijing, 2015, p. 9.

role in improving people's character and realizing their comprehensive development. "People differ in talent, but all need to learn,"[1] as a saying goes. Marx conceptualized the role of education from the perspective of productive labor, and he understood education as an important way to improve the competence and character of the worker. He noted, "[I]n order to modify the human organism, so that it may acquire skill and handiness in a given branch of industry, and become labor-power of a special kind, a special education or training is requisite."[2] Education can help people acquire new knowledge, new skills, and new abilities; improve their morals; enhance their scientific and cultural competence; strengthen their comprehensive capabilities and innovative thinking; empower them to develop themselves, contribute to society, and benefit the people.

In modern society, science and technology play an ever more prominent role in developing productive forces and have become the primary productive force. Accordingly, improving education has become a prerequisite for increasing social production, and education is becoming an important way to improve people's character and promote their comprehensive development. Xi Jinping has emphasized that we should focus not only on the acquisition of scientific knowledge through education but also on the cultivation of morals. We should educate and guide the people to establish a sound attitude toward health and to improve their health. We should educate the people by virtue of aesthetics and culture. Moreover, we should carry forward the spirit of labor and foster a social environment in which labor is loved and respected.

---

1 Cited from *A Comparative Study of Different Schools of Learning* by Wang Chong (27-c. 97) of the Eastern Han dynasty (25-220).
2 Karl Marx: *Capital*, Vol. I, Progress Publishers, Moscow, 1995, p. 121.

## 1.2 Education: the cornerstone of national rejuvenation and social progress

General Secretary Xi has always approached education from the perspective of socio-economic development. When he worked in Fujian province, he examined the relationships between the economy, science, technology, talent, and education, and emphasized the fundamental role of education. "The economy relies on science and technology, which in turn depends on talent, and talent relies on education. Educational advancement, technological progress, and economic revitalization make up a complementary, sequential, and unified process, the foundation of which lies in education."[1]

Education can provide the talent needed for national rejuvenation and social progress. An old saying goes, "The key to governance of a country lies in talent."[2] Throughout the ages, talented individuals have underpinned the prosperity of states. Achievements are realized because of talent. Such individuals build solid foundations for great causes. They are important drivers of modern economic growth and social progress. They are creators and disseminators of advanced productive forces and culture, and thus they represent an important force that plays a fundamental, strategic, and decisive role in economic and social development. Whichever country can train more talent will gain strategic advantages in economic and social development and will take a leading position in international competition. In today's world, human resources are becoming even more important, as they are a key driver of economic and social advancement. Education is fundamental to training talent. We have no reason not to rely on education. As the times advance, the significance of knowledge and talent has never become so apparent, and thus the status and role of education grow in importance.

Education can provide an innovative impetus for national rejuvenation and social progress. The driving forces behind development

---

1 Xi Jinping: *Up and Out of Poverty*, Foreign Languages Press, Beijing, 2016, p. 180.
2 Cited from *A Collection of Short Essays on Education at Songzi County* by Hu Yuan (993-1059) of the Northern Song dynasty (960-1127).

determine its speed, efficiency, and sustainability, and innovation is the primary driving force for development. To pursue innovation is to pursue development, and to seek innovation is to plan for the future. "The history of human development proves that innovation has always been important for promoting the development of a country and its people as well as human society."[1] In today's world, science and technology are advancing rapidly, and international competition is becoming fierce. Having experienced the Global Financial Crisis of 2007-2008, which was an unusual event, countries have adjusted their development strategies and paid more attention to scientific and technological progress, as well as innovation-driven development. Scientific and technological innovation has become key for enhancing overall national strength, and played a powerful role in guiding the transformation and progress of ways of life and economic activity. Whichever country leads scientific and technological innovation can gain a competitive edge. Thus, we should vigorously develop education to meet strategic national needs. We should increase innovations, develop new technologies, invent new tools of production, and accelerate the application of science and technology in production. This way, we can promote large-scale, high-level development of social production, and provide continuous drive and support for national revitalization and social progress.

## 1.3 Education: an important force for sustaining human civilization and creating a better life

Education is an important force for advancing human civilization. The history of human development shows that education has led to progress from generation to generation. Every country and every nation has arrived where it is today by building on the past and embarking for the future. The world has become what it is today through the

---

1 Xi Jinping: *The Governance of China*, Vol. II, Foreign Languages Press, Beijing, 2017, p. 292.

inheritance, creation, exchange, and integration of various human civilizations. Civilization is the soul of a country and a nation. The civilization of every country and nation is context-specific and thus unique. Any civilization, regardless of its territorial, national, and social origins, needs inheritance, innovation, communication, and mutual learning. This is an important law governing the development of civilizations. In this process, education has played an important role in not only inheriting and carrying forward the best part of traditional culture and outstanding achievements of human civilization, but also recreating past knowledge—which might still be relevant today despite being expressed in outdated forms—with modern meaning and expression. This way, we can bring out the vitality of this knowledge and realize the preservation, creation, and progress of civilizations.

Education is essential to meeting people's growing desire for a better life. A better life is a universal goal and a common aspiration of humanity. Pursuing this goal is an inexhaustible driving force for the survival and development of humanity and the progress of human civilization. The creation of a better life is the common aspiration of the people in China and elsewhere. To that end, education represents an important approach to promoting economic and social development while improving people's lives. It is also an important way to enrich spiritual life and improve the overall quality of life. Education is integral to guaranteeing basic survival, sound living conditions, and satisfactory work for all members of society. In 2013, in his video message for the first anniversary of the UN Global Education First Initiative, Xi Jinping emphasized that China will show firm resolve in implementing its strategy for revitalizing the country through science and education, as it has always made education a strategic priority. China will increase its investment in education, promote education for all and lifelong education, and turn itself into a learning society. Moreover, the country will work hard to ensure that every child has the opportunity to attend school, and it will enable its 1.3 billion people to enjoy better and fairer education.

## 2. Education as a Major Undertaking of the State and the Party

Education is the foundation of a country's development in the long run. Based on China's national conditions, General Secretary Xi has accurately identified the historic challenges and opportunities facing China in the new era. Thus, he proposed at the National Education Conference that education is the great mission of the nation and the Communist Party of China. As an organic whole, this great mission contributes to the development of socialism with Chinese characteristics, as well as the realization of the Chinese Dream of national rejuvenation and the building of a great, modern socialist country. This innovative idea highlights the prominent role of education in all areas of undertakings of the Party and the state, providing the fundamental rationale for implementing the strategy of prioritizing education in the new era.

---

### ❦ Quote from Xi Jinping ❦

Education is the cornerstone of national rejuvenation and social progress, and it is a benevolent project that will benefit generations to come. It plays a decisive role in improving the nation's character, promoting the comprehensive development of individuals, enhancing China's creativity and innovative capacity, and realizing the rejuvenation of the Chinese nation.

—Speech at the National Education Conference, September 10, 2018

---

### 2.1 Education: a cause that will benefit generations to come

It takes ten years to grow a tree, but it takes decades to bring up talent. What kind of talent our education system should produce is of fundamental importance because education determines the future. Education does not produce immediate results and should not be too utilitarian. Instead, we should have a long-term strategic vision and make continuous, unrelenting efforts. Valuing education equates to valuing the future. Only by ensuring high-quality and competitive education can we win the future. More so than any other undertaking, education today influences and even determines the training of our new generations for the socialist cause, as well as the long-term stability of our country, national rejuvenation, and national prosperity. Only by vigorously developing education and cultivating capable young people well prepared to join the socialist cause and well equipped with a comprehensive moral, intellectual, physical, and aesthetic grounding, as well as a love for labor, can we ensure that this mission of the Party and the nation is passed on to and carried forward by our new generations for the socialist cause.

Education affects the wellbeing of the people, as well as social equity and national rejuvenation. Education is a shared mission of the CPC, the country, and all the people in China. Education supplies talent for economic and social development and shapes the future of every family and every child. It is an important way to improve people's wellbeing and to promote social equity and justice. It provides important support for the building of a moderately prosperous society in all respects and the building of China into a great modern socialist country. Xi Jinping has emphasized that education plays a decisive role in enhancing the innovative capacity of the Chinese nation and realizing the rejuvenation of the Chinese nation. Education is, in the final analysis, the key to achieving the Two Centenary Goals and realizing the Chinese Dream of national rejuvenation. Therefore, education must be given a more prominent strategic position.

## 2.2 The fundamental, guiding, and all-encompassing role of education in modernization drive

In the drive for modernization, education plays a fundamental, guiding, and all-encompassing role. As an undertaking that focuses on cultivating people, education is future-oriented. The development of all areas of society is rooted in talent training. Education should be farsighted, as it should not only meet the needs of the present but also consider the requirements of the future. Education has a long development cycle, and its effects are felt over the long run. Thus, education should meet the various requirements of the socialist drive for modernization. It should also enjoy early development and play a guiding role in social development as it fundamentally shapes all sectors and the destiny of the country and its people.

As socialism with Chinese characteristics has entered a new era, the fundamental, guiding, and all-encompassing role of education has become more prominent. The further modernization progresses, the higher the requirements for talent training and the more prominent the role of education becomes. As we progress toward a multi-polar world, an IT-based society, economic globalization, and cultural diversity, education is increasingly intertwined with economic and social advancement, and its modernization is becoming more important for the modernization of the country.

To achieve the Two Centenary Goals and realize the Chinese Dream of national rejuvenation, we must pay more attention to education. China is getting closer to the world's center stage, and it is closer than ever to realizing national rejuvenation. The period between the 19th CPC National Congress held in 2017 and the year 2020 will be decisive for finishing the building of a moderately prosperous society in all respects. And the period between the 19th and the 20th CPC National Congresses is the period of transition from the First to the Second Centenary Goal. We must finish building a moderately prosperous society in all respects and achieve the First Centenary Goal. Similarly, we must build upon our past achievements and embark upon a new journey of making China a modern socialist country while striving to realize the Second Centenary Goal. In this current era, development is the top priority. To that end, people are the most important resources, and innovation is its greatest driving force. This new era has presented an urgent need for scientific knowledge and brilliant minds. To achieve the Two Centenary Goals, we must give greater play to the supporting role of education.

# 3. Giving Strategic Priority to Education

"Respecting and advocating education is an essential foundation of the country. Valuing and training talent is the first priority for governance," said the Ming-dynasty scholar Zhu Zhiyu. In the 1980s when Xi Jinping worked in Zhengding county, Hebei province, he was informed by the local people that the most run-down buildings in many villages were their schools. Thus, he inspected the classrooms and dormitories of Beijiacun Primary School and found that the school was in a state of disrepair. He said to the village officials, "We must ensure that the best building in the village is its school." After that, he asked the county Party committee to issue a notice that required all townships and villages to work toward this goal. To keep track of the state of these dilapidated school buildings and the progress toward their renovation, he visited the schools whenever he could find the time. As a result, the county raised 1.87 million yuan to improve the conditions of its schools. In addition, it repaired or rebuilt 1,020 dilapidated classrooms, purchased more than 3,000 sets of wooden desks and chairs for students, and constructed new teaching buildings for 16 villages. Later, when he worked in Fujian, Zhejiang, and Shanghai, Xi Jinping always emphasized the importance of prioritizing education from the strategic perspective of economic and social development. At the National Education Conference, he further pointed out that we should continue to prioritize education to advance the cause of the CPC and the state. We should continue to make education conform to the needs of the CPC, the country, the expectations of the people, China's overall national strength, and its international standing.

## 3.1 Invigorating China through science, education, and talent

Implementing the strategies for invigorating China through science and education and for developing a quality workforce is a major strategy of the CPC Central Committee. It was applied during the course of reform and opening up, and throughout the drive for modernization, on the basis of comprehensive analysis of domestic and international circumstances, as well as China's overall development. Since reform and opening up, our Party has successively implemented the national strategies of invigorating the country through science, education, sustainable development, and the development of a quality workforce. The Party has also initiated an early start for education modernization, and it has relied on education modernization to support national modernization, which is a long-term mechanism in the making.

Invigorating China through science and education is an important national strategy. Deng Xiaoping repeatedly emphasized the important role of education throughout the socialist drive for modernization, and he regarded education as a fundamental undertaking that influences all aspects of this drive, as well as the future of socialism. He pointed out, "We should try every way to expand education, even if it means slowing down in other fields."[1] When he proposed the three-step strategy for achieving socialist modernization in China, Deng believed that education, science, and technology should be prioritized. He pointed out that to realize modernization, science and technology are the key, and education is the foundation. Thanks to his initiative, the 12th CPC National Congress in 1982 first identified education as one of the strategic priorities in China's modernization drive.

Jiang Zemin pointed out that we should prioritize strategies for invigorating China through science, education, and sustainable development. He believed that in a country with such a large population and a relative shortage of resources, which was relatively backward in economic and cultural development, the decisive step to achieve the grand goals of national rejuvenation and socialist modernization would be to implement a strategy for invigorating the country through science and technology. To develop economy, we should leverage scientific and technological progress and improve the quality of the workforce. To

---

1 Deng Xiaoping: *Selected Works of Deng Xiaoping*, Vol. III, Foreign Languages Press, Beijing, 1994, p. 270.

strategically prioritize education is essential to accomplishing China's modernization drive.

In this new century, facing new changes at home and abroad, the central government has put forward a strategy for building a quality workforce. Hu Jintao said that we must show firm resolve in implementing a strategy for invigorating China through science and education while also building a quality workforce. We must always take the training of high-caliber talent as our fundamental task, and we must give strategic priority to education.

Implementing the strategies to rejuvenate the country through science, education, and talent is critical for socialism with Chinese characteristics in the new era. General Secretary Xi has pointed out that with its large population, vast territory, and wide regional gaps, China faces an arduous task in developing its education system. Although China has already become the second largest economy in the world, it is still the largest developing country and is still at the initial stage of socialism. We face a shortage of various educational resources, unbalanced educational provision across different regions, and suboptimal educational conditions. The incomes of teachers, especially those working at the grassroots level, are generally insufficient, and the conditions and standards for operating educational institutions are unsatisfactory. Likewise, education management needs to be improved. Against this background, we must be committed to these strategies by prioritizing education, so as to improve and strengthen our education through reform. The report to the 18th CPC National Congress states that we should "pursue at a faster pace the strategy of training competent personnel as a priority to build a large contingent of such personnel, and turn China from a country with large human resources into one with a large pool of competent professionals."[1] The report to the 19th CPC National Congress states, "We must show firm resolve in implementing the strategy for invigorating

---

1 Hu Jintao: "Firmly March on the Path of Socialism with Chinese Characteristics and Strive to Complete the Building of a Moderately Prosperous Society in All Respects—Report to the Eighteenth National Congress of the Communist Party of China," *Qiushi Journal*, October-December 2012, p. 55.

China through science and education, the strategy on developing a quality workforce…"[1] From the strategic perspective of adhering to and developing socialism with Chinese characteristics for the new era, the report makes major strategic commitments to the priority position of education and to the transformation of the country into a modern educational powerhouse.

## 3.2 Improving the mechanism for prioritizing education

To implement the strategic plan for prioritizing education, we must approach education in the context of economic and social development. We must position it in relation to the rejuvenation of the Chinese nation, as well as the needs of the country, and we must make educational plans that conform with the expectations of the people. To improve our systems and mechanisms for prioritizing education, we should put education first in government support, development planning, and resources allocation. We must ensure that education is prioritized in economic and social development planning and in the allocation of fiscal expenditures. Moreover, we should ensure that education and human resources development are prioritized in the allocation of public resources.

Education should be given priority in economic and social development plans. This requires us to put education first throughout the strategic planning of developing Chinese socialism in the new era, align educational planning with economic and social planning, and formulate realistic goals and policies. We must incorporate overall development planning of education into economic and social plans and policies. Since the Third Plenary Session of the 18th CPC Central Committee held in 2013, the meetings of the Central Leading Group for Deepening Reform, and the Central Commission for Deepening Reform,

---

1 Xi Jinping: "Secure a Decisive Victory in Building a Moderately Prosperous Society in All Respects and Strive for the Great Success of Socialism with Chinese Characteristics for a New Era," *The Governance of China*, Vol. III, Foreign Languages Press, Beijing, 2020, p. 29.

chaired by Xi Jinping, have reviewed and approved many policy documents, in addition to producing practical and informed top-level designs for relevant work, so that the education-first concept is translated into practice. Party committees and governments at all levels must strengthen planning and play more proactive leadership roles. In addition, they must prioritize educational planning so that the two strategic tasks—accelerating education modernization and turning China into a country strong in education—can be operationalized as policies and measures that can be implemented, monitored, and evaluated. Efforts must be made to modernize educational concepts, systems, institutions, content, methods, and governance, thus supporting economic and social development.

Funding for education should be prioritized. Education investment plays a fundamental and strategic role in supporting long-term national development, and it has become an important indicator for evaluating whether a country or region prioritizes education. Investment guarantees the priority status of education. Government expenditure on education as percentage of GDP is internationally recognized as an important indicator for measuring the quality and strength of education. In 2012, China made a historic breakthrough in its investment in education, with government expenditure on education reaching 4% of its GDP for the first time, a level that has been maintained ever since. *China's Education Modernization 2035*[1] further points out that government expenditure on education as percentage of GDP should be no less than 4%. It also states that the general public budget for education as a whole and per enrolled student should increase year on year. Moreover, we should extend reform of education investment mechanisms and put in place a statutory, standardized, institutionalized, and evidence-based system for education investment, as well as a mechanism for allocating,

---

1 At the end of 2018, the CPC Central Committee and the State Council issued *China's Education Modernization 2035*. As the first medium- and long-term plan on modernizing the education system, it specifies the strategic goals, tasks, and measures for implementation. It is a master plan for turning the country into an educational powerhouse in the new era.

utilizing, and managing funds used for education.

Priority to education requires more spending on education, which is key to an improved public fiscal system. It is necessary to clarify the responsibilities of governments at all levels regarding education expenditure. In addition, a stable and sustainable education investment system that is compatible with the socialist market economy and that meets the needs of public education must be established. We must ensure that in the allocation of government spending, statutory increases in funding for public education should be prioritized. Governments at all levels should prioritize education in their fiscal spending. They should drive education investment through better design of policies, systems, and standards, and improve the long-term mechanisms to ensure the sustained and stable growth of government expenditure on education.

In the allocation of public resources, the needs of education and human resources should be met first. Priority to education requires improved systems of resource allocation, more emphasis on education and human resources development, and faster accumulation of human capital through greater investment. We must meet the needs of both economic development and the people, and we must effectively coordinate and utilize all educational resources, focus on ensuring basic educational resources, strengthen weak areas in education investment, and promote educational equality. We should channel more public educational resources to regions, schools, sectors, and groups facing difficulties in accessing education. We should promote coordinated development between urban and rural areas and between regions, and strive to improve the coverage and quality of basic public services.

## 3.3 Delivering quality education as the responsibility of the entire society

Education affects the vital interests of countless families, the future of the country, and its people. It is a systematic undertaking that requires the participation of multiple forces. Xi Jinping pointed out at the National Education Conference that families, schools, government, and society should all do their share and perform their responsibilities in education. Only when society at large attaches great importance to education, and only when families, schools, government, and society work closely together to create a healthy environment conducive to the growth and development of young people, can we better realize the prioritized development of education.

The responsibilities of families should be emphasized as the first step for society at large to create synergy for educational success. As the cells of society, families serve as the first schools. Xi Jinping has emphasized that parents are their children's first teachers and thus should teach them the "first lessons of life" and help them get off to a good start in life. Among the many aspects of family education, the most important is character-building. If we fail to sow good seeds in the first place, no matter how much we cultivate the land, it will be difficult to reap a good harvest. Parents should pass on good moral values to their children, cultivating in them integrity and compassion, and preparing them to serve the country and the people. Parents should teach their children to appreciate the true, the good, and the beautiful, and to avoid the false, the evil, and the ugly. Moreover, parents should respect the educational arrangements of schools and the creative efforts of teachers. They should cooperate with schools to ensure that their children receive a good education. Also, parents should pay close attention to psychological and behavioral changes in their children, and guide them in the right developmental paths. In addition, educational departments and women's federations should coordinate social resources to support family education.

All segments of society should care about education, create a good educational environment, and shoulder the responsibility of nurturing young people. Society is a big classroom, and life is a textbook. Social education should be strengthened through multiple channels, such as newspapers, television, radio, new media, theaters, cinemas, and street bulletin boards, to foster a good educational atmosphere in which families, schools, government, and society work together. Various public, cultural, and educational service providers share the mission with families and schools to help children build moral character. With the increasing wealth of civil society, there are numerous social resources available that should be fully tapped. We should improve the policy for the effective allocation and development of society's educational resources, and step up efforts to build public facilities such as libraries, museums, science and technology centers, memorial halls, stadiums, children's palaces, and activity centers. Such facilities should provide conditions for students to understand society and take part in social practices. Furthermore, public agencies, institutions, and state-owned enterprises should establish integrity- and competence-based employment and promotion mechanisms to set good examples for society at large by shouldering the social responsibility of education.

Party committees and governments at all levels should put the reform and development of education on their agenda, and improve relevant systems and mechanisms for reform and innovation. They should guarantee the safety and security of schools to relieve them of any concerns, and protect the dignity of teachers and schools, and the safety of students. General Secretary Xi has emphasized that Party committees and governments at all levels should strategically prioritize education, strengthen the sense of responsibility, and address problems in education reform and development in a timely manner. Leading Party and government officials should understand and care about education, and carry out educational research. They should focus on key issues and problems in education, intensify institutional reforms, and fully unleash the vitality of education.

# Chapter 4

## Socialist Characteristics of China's Education System

The direction in which we are heading determines the path we take, and the path we take determines our future. The direction we take in education affects whether or not we achieve success in education. It also affects the comprehensive development of socialist modernization. General Secretary Xi Jinping has unequivocally stated that our education should follow the guidance of Marxism and serve the people, the CPC governance of China, socialism with Chinese characteristics, reform and opening up, and socialist modernization. These statements have answered the fundamental question of how to ensure the success of socialist education with Chinese characteristics, pointing out the correct political direction for the reform and development of education in the new era.

# 1. Adhering to Socialist Education

Xi Jinping has emphasized the vital importance of the direction of education. He has pointed out on many occasions that China is a socialist country led by the CPC, and we should thus adhere to socialist education and follow the guidance of Marxism. On this issue, we must be clear-headed and firm in our position and attitude, leaving no room for any ambiguity.

## 1.1 Setting the right direction to ensure good education

At all times and all over the world, every country trains its talent according to its own political philosophy. As Xi Jinping has stated, "There are many schools of thought and different theoretical views on education, but they all share the belief that education must train people for social development."[1] Specifically, this is about the accumulation of knowledge, cultural preservation, national survival, and policy implementation. Therefore, education is at all times closely related to the political philosophy of a country, and it continues to develop and strengthen itself by serving the development of the country.

China's education is socialist in nature, as determined by the nature of the country. The Constitution provides that the People's Republic of China is a socialist state under the people's democratic rule—led by the working class and based on an alliance of workers and farmers—and has thus developed socialist education. The Education Law of the People's Republic

---

1 Xi Jinping: *Speech at the Meeting with Teachers and Students of Peking University*, Chinese edition, People's Publishing House, Beijing, 2018, p. 5.

of China provides that the basic principles set out in the Constitution should be followed to develop socialist education. This is the fundamental basis for our adherence to the socialist direction in education.

The direction of education determines its purposes and approaches. What kind of people to cultivate is the first question that education must answer. A school that takes the wrong direction in educating its students is like a crooked tree that will never grow tall. The values of young students determine the values of the future of society at large, as well as the long-term competitiveness of the Chinese nation, and they put at stake whether or not socialism with Chinese characteristics can be carried forward by our new generations of socialist builders. Xi Jinping has emphasized that education in China should train a new generation of capable young people who are well-prepared participants of the socialist cause instead of bystanders or, worse still, opponents and gravediggers. Therefore, the direction of education is of fundamental importance. Taking a wrong direction will lead us further away from our goal. Nothing is more crucial than training new generations for the socialist cause, and nothing is more dangerous than things going wrong in this respect. In education, there is every reason to emphasize the correct political direction and socialist education should naturally adhere to a socialist direction.

## 1.2 Taking a firm position on the direction of education

Under new circumstances, we now face new challenges in upholding the socialist direction of education. The world is undergoing major development, transformation, and adjustment, and China is at a crucial stage in its transformation from a large country to a strong one. The external environment has become more complex, as certain countries and international forces increase pressure on us out of fear and in order to contain us. Xi Jinping has pointed out that the entire Party must remain clear-headed about which flag to raise and which path to follow. Hostile forces at home and abroad have been trying to undermine our Party, attempting to make us abandon our belief in Marxism, socialism, and communism. "Some people, even some Party members, have failed to see through their hidden agenda. They argue why we could not accept the 'universal values' that have developed in the West over hundreds of years, along with certain Western political concepts. They argue no harm will be done if we do. Some even regard Western theories and discourse as the golden rule and thus unconsciously become trumpeters of Western capitalist ideology."[1] For this reason, confusion has been caused in some people's understanding of the socialist direction of education. If we fail to clear up such confusion in a timely manner, socialist education will suffer heavy losses, and we will fail to ensure a steady supply of capable young people to carry forward socialism with Chinese characteristics.

On the direction of education, we must never hesitate to take a clear stance and resort to firm action. Xi Jinping has emphasized that we must remain clear-headed to improve and develop China's socialist system. In addition, we must unswervingly follow the path of socialism with Chinese characteristics. We must continue to uphold the guiding position of Marxism in education and spare no effort to advocate and disseminate Marxism. We must practice the core socialist values throughout the whole process of education, and guide teachers and students to be firm believers, active communicators, and model practitioners of these values. We must conscientiously implement a responsibility system for ideological work, follow the guidance of Marxism, and integrate all constructive ideas and cultures into our mainstream ideology. Furthermore, we must create a good political and educational environment and prevent erroneous thinking from infiltrating institutes of education, thus ensuring that schools are harmonious, stable, clean, and upright.

## 2. Following the Guidance of Marxism

Xi Jinping has always been committed to studying Marxism. In

---

1 Xi Jinping: *Speech at the National Conference on Party Schools*, Chinese edition, People's Publishing House, Beijing, 2016, p. 8.

the seven years he spent in the countryside as an educated youth, he read *Das Kapital* three times under a kerosene lamp in a cave dwelling and wrote 18 thick volumes of notes. Regardless of where he was—working and living with farmers on the Loess Plateau at Liangjiahe village in Shaanxi province, or working in local or central governments—he persevered in reading Marxist classics. When presiding over the drafting of the report to the 18th CPC National Congress, he specifically asked for the following statement to be included, "Communists' faith in Marxism, socialism, and communism is their political soul and sustains them in all tests." In December 2016, during the National Conference on Moral and Political Work in Institutions of Higher Learning, he stated that to manage education well and to adhere to the direction of socialist education, we must follow the guidance of Marxism, implement the CPC's education policy, publicize Marxist theory, and ensure a quality Marxist education to lay the ideological foundation for students' lifelong growth.

---

### ❧ *Quote from Xi Jinping* ❧

Marxism is the fundamental guiding philosophy upon which our Party and our country are founded, and it is what makes Chinese universities unique.

—Speech at the meeting with teachers and students of Peking University, May 2, 2018

---

## 2.1 Marxism making China's education unique

Marxism is the fundamental guiding philosophy upon which our Party and our country are founded. Chairman Mao Zedong said, "A doctrine is like a flag: only when a flag is raised does everyone have hope and a sense of purpose."[1] Marxism is a scientific theory that

---

1  Party Literature Research Office of the CPC Central Committee *et al.*, eds.: *Mao Zedong's Early Manuscripts (June 1912-November 1920)*, Chinese edition, People's Publishing House, Beijing, 1990, p. 554.

creatively reveals the laws that underlie the evolution of human society and shows the way for humanity to leap from the kingdom of necessity to the kingdom of freedom. Marxism is the theory for the people, and it was the first to create an ideological system for the people in their ideological self-liberation. Based on scientific theories, it points out the direction for the ultimate establishment of an ideal society free from oppression and exploitation, where everyone is equal and free. Marxism is an applied theory. It guides people's actions to change the world. It is formed, enriched, and developed in the people's practice of self-liberation, and it provides the people with strong intellectual support to understand and transform the world. Marxism is an inclusive theory. It has always been a cutting-edge philosophy developed in response to real-world changes. It has continuously explored new developmental questions and has responded in kind to new challenges facing human society.

As Marxism has profoundly transformed the world, it has profoundly transformed China. The destiny of Marxism has been closely linked with that of the Communist Party of China, the Chinese people, and the Chinese nation from the outset. Here in China, Marxism's rationality and truthfulness has been fully tested, its people-centric and practical nature fully revealed, and its open-ended and contemporary nature fully demonstrated. Moreover, experience has proven that Marxism has been a strong theoretical tool for China's revolution, development, and reform, enabling the country to create an unprecedented miracle of development. Xi Jinping has stated, "It is entirely proper that history and the people have chosen Marxism, and it is entirely proper that the Communist Party of China has inscribed Marxism on its banner. It is also entirely proper that we continue to integrate the fundamental tenets of Marxism with China's specific realities, just as we continue to adapt Marxism to China's conditions, and keep it current."[1] Marxism has always been the guiding philosophy of our Party and our state, and it has been a powerful ideological

---

1 Xi Jinping: *Speech at the Ceremony Commemorating the Bicentennial of the Birth of Karl Marx*, Chinese edition, People's Publishing House, Beijing, 2018, pp. 14-15.

weapon for us to understand and transform the world.

Marxism has been chosen by history and the people as the unique feature of socialist education in China. It has also become the banner and soul of education reform and development in China. Socialist education must follow the guidance of Marxism. Otherwise, our education will lose its soul and direction. On this issue, the overwhelming majority of the people are sober-minded and maintain a firm attitude. Nonetheless, nebulous or erroneous notions still exist among some people. For example, some think that Marxism is obsolete and the theory followed in China is no longer Marxism. And some argue that Marxism is nothing but ideological preaching, devoid of scientific principles or academic rigor. Marxism is marginalized, trivialized, and stereotyped in certain realms; it has disappeared from the textbooks in some fields of study, no longer heard in academic discussions and debates. These issues must not go unnoticed.

To follow the guidance of Marxism, we should earnestly study it, understand it, believe in it, and put it into practice. Only by truly understanding Marxism can we truly believe in it and become more vigilant in resisting all kinds of erroneous thinking. To follow the guidance of Marxism, the key is to answer the question "for whom." To strengthen our socialist education, we must remain people-centered throughout the development of education. To follow the guidance of Marxism, we should focus on its application in addressing the major theoretical and practical issues regarding the development of education in China, and we should use it to propose questions and then find their answers.

## 2.2 Marxist theory as the ideological foundation for students' lifelong growth

Education should serve as a stronghold for studying, researching, and disseminating Marxism, and for making the theme of Marxism even more prominent. Colleges and universities should fully exercise their own strengths, reinforce the study of Marxism, and establish better Marxist schools and disciplines. We should build upon the practice of developing socialism with Chinese characteristics, provide in-depth answers to major theoretical and practical questions, and promote Marxism in contemporary China and in the 21st century. Moreover, we must resolutely train experienced Marxist scholars with firm positions and academic rigor, including in particular, a large number of young Marxists. Effective reform measures should be taken to prevent the "marginalization" of the research and teaching of Marxism in colleges and universities. Furthermore, Marxist schools in institutes of higher learning should follow Marxism as their guiding political and educational principle, and make their due contribution toward consolidating Marxism as the guiding ideology in China while ensuring the inclusion of Marxism in textbooks and classroom teaching and its being understood by students.

We should persistently spread Marxist theory and further refine Marxist education. Xi Jinping has emphasized that Marxist education must be enhanced to deepen students' understanding of Marxism's historical necessity, its truthful nature, and its theoretical and practical significance. Throughout this process, students should be taught to apply Marxist standpoints, outlook, and methodologies to observe and analyze the world. They should also be taught to clarify the missions of the current era and to identify development trends in China and in the world so that they can fully appreciate the power of the truth of Marxism. Moreover, students from all disciplines and at all stages of learning should understand Marxist theory, and adopt the Marxist worldview and scientific methodology, to lay a foundation for their growth and development. At the same time, educators should be able to localize Marxist theory and explain them in a way accessible to students, turn basic theories into lively arguments and fundamental methodologies into applicable methods, and cater to the general and individual needs of students.

We should study and practice Marxism, and draw sagacious wisdom and theoretical strength from it. At the Ceremony Commemorating the Bicentennial of the Birth of Karl Marx, Xi Jinping stated that we should study and adopt the Marxist thought on: the laws of social development; putting people first; productive forces and production relations; the people's democracy; cultural and social advancement; the relationship between people and nature; world history; and the development of a Marxist political party. He noted that we need to use Marxist world-view and methodology to observe and interpret the world today and lead us through the times, while developing Marxism through dynamic and diversified practices in contemporary China. We should learn from all the achievements of human civilization with an extensive view. To outdo ourselves we need to base on our tradition while making innovations, and learn widely from the strengths of others. Finally, we need to have a deeper understanding of governance by a communist party, the development of socialism, and the evolution of human society, and open up new prospects for the development of Marxism in contemporary China and in the 21st century.

We should arm teachers and students with the latest theoretical achievements in adapting Marxism to China. Xi Jinping Thought on Socialism with Chinese Characteristics for a New Era is the latest of such achievements. Taking into consideration the characteristics of students in different stages of learning, we should guide teachers and students to study this thought in an in-depth, systematic, and timely fashion so that their learning, understanding, and application of this thought can be integrated, and their understanding of, belief in, and practice of it can be consistent. We should coordinate our efforts in the study and research of this thought to publicize and explain its background, historic status, rich content, systematicness, and essence. Moreover, we should further our understanding of its development context, theoretical framework, and practical value, cultivating a clear theoretical understanding, a firm political belief, and a scientific approach to thinking.

## 3. Commitment to the Four Purposes of Education

In December 2016, Xi Jinping proposed at the National Conference on Moral and Political Work in Institutions of Higher Learning that we should be committed to the four purposes of education. He stated that the development of higher education in China must be aligned with the current targets and future direction of national development, emphasizing that our education should serve the people, the governance of the CPC, the consolidation and development of socialism with Chinese characteristics, reform and opening up, and socialist modernization. Should we deviate from these purposes, higher education would lose its foundations and find it hard to succeed. At the National Education Conference and the Meeting with Teachers of Moral and Political Theory, he emphasized that we must adhere to socialist education and be committed to its four purposes.

## 3.1 Education for serving the people

The Communist Party of China was born from the people, is rooted in the people, and serves the people. Thus, it always puts the people's interests first. Prosperity for the people is the basic political position of the CPC, and it is the prominent feature that distinguishes Marxist parties from other ones. It is also an intrinsic requirement for the Party to maintain its progressive nature and its integrity. Education is an important undertaking of the CPC. Serving the people through education reflects the basic principle of serving the people wholeheartedly. Xi Jinping has stated that it is the people who create history and that China's communists should never forget this basic principle of historical materialism.

To ensure that education serves the people, we must focus on realizing, maintaining, and developing the fundamental interests of the overwhelming majority of the Chinese people, and we must continue to meet the people's needs for better education at a higher level. This requires the education sector to be people-centered. It also requires us to identify the evolving problems in Chinese society while enabling all people in China to share fully and fairly the benefits of educational development. To ensure that education serves the people, we must make every effort to address the gravest needs and problems of the people, and we must solve their most pressing concerns, as well as those that are essential to their immediate interests. We should satisfy the needs of the people and make solid efforts to address their concerns so that they will always have a strong sense of gain, happiness, and security. To ensure that education serves the people, we must be one with the people and regard them as our teachers, thus aligning our respect for the laws of social and educational development with the principal status of the people. Moreover, we should extensively pool the practical wisdom of the people to gain their broadest support and rely on them to open up new prospects for education reform and development.

## 3.2 Education for serving the CPC governance

Ensuring that education serves the CPC governance is a fundamental requirement for adhering to and developing socialism with Chinese characteristics. It is also a practical necessity for consolidating our Party's governance, improving its capacity to govern, ensuring its long-term governance, and guaranteeing the long-term stability of the country.

To ensure that education serves the CPC governance, we must adhere to the basic principle, unite our people, nurture the younger generations, foster cultural prosperity, publicize our image, and consolidate our Party's governance. The education sector should take the lead in adapting Marxism to the Chinese context in keeping with the times, enhancing its popular appeal, and developing a strong socialist ideology. Educators should foster solidarity among the people in terms of their beliefs, values, and ethics, and ensure that Xi Jinping Thought on Socialism with Chinese Characteristics for a New Era is embraced by the people. We should educate and guide people of all ethnic groups to enhance their sense of identity with the motherland, the Chinese nation and culture, the Communist Party of China, and socialism with Chinese characteristics. We should also strengthen their sense of national identity and patriotism. This way, people from all ethnic groups will cherish and protect ethnic solidarity, just as they cherish their own eyes and lives, thus sharing in the historic mission of national rejuvenation and the great cause of national prosperity. Through education, we must unite all social groups, maintain the Party's close ties with the people, and attract the best talent inside and outside the Party, from both home and abroad, to partake in the great endeavors of the Party and the state, thus fostering stronger public support for governance by the Party. We should give full play to the important role of education in grassroots Party organizations, thus continuing the consolidation of the organizational foundations for governance by the Party. Moreover, we must care about, respect, and unite intellectuals while creating better conditions for their work and study. In addition, we should accelerate the development of systems and mechanisms conducive to the entrepreneurial endeavors of intellectuals so that they are able to concentrate on their professional careers, fully tap into their talent, and fully unleash their energy.

To ensure that education serves the governance of the Communist Party of China, we must improve the capacity of the Party to carry out the great struggle for national development, the great project of strengthening our Party, the great cause of Chinese socialism, and to realize the great dream of national rejuvenation. We must strengthen the education of Party officials to enable them to be politically strong and highly competent, so as to develop a team of high-caliber, professional Party officials while also building our Party characterized by its study of Marxism. Through education, we must ensure that our Party learns well and properly exercises political leadership, reform, and innovation. We must also ensure that it promotes sound development, exercises law-based governance, engages with the people, implements policies, and manages risks. Moreover, we must ensure that our Party can always stand ahead of the times throughout its historical journey amid profound changes worldwide, and we must ensure that it can always act as the backbone of the Chinese people throughout their historical response to domestic and international risks, as well as tests of all kinds. Finally, we must ensure that it can always be the strong core source of leadership throughout this historical journey of adhering to and developing Chinese socialism.

### 3.3 Education for serving the consolidation and development of socialism with Chinese characteristics

Ensuring that education serves the consolidation and development of socialism with Chinese characteristics is an important task for socialist education. It is also an important reflection of socialist education, and an essential requirement for upholding, developing, consolidating, and improving Chinese socialism. Chinese socialism represents a fundamental institutional guarantee for progress and development in China today. It is an advanced system with distinct Chinese features, remarkable institutional strengths, and a strong capacity for self-improvement. This system suits China, and it upholds the essence of socialism while drawing upon the constructive achievements of institutional development across the whole world and throughout history. Moreover, it reflects the characteristics and strengths of Chinese socialism and is therefore unique and effective. We should be aware, however, that the system is not yet perfect. Today, we are tasked with the important historic mission of making socialism with Chinese characteristics more mature and better established. We are also tasked with providing a set of complete, more stable, and more effective systems for the development of the Party and the country, social harmony and stability, and the enduring prosperity and stability of the country. Likewise, education should also follow this trend, with full confidence in socialism with Chinese characteristics while serving its consolidation and development.

To ensure that education serves the consolidation and development of Chinese socialism, we should guide our people along with educational development and enhance their confidence and conviction in both China's political system and the common ideal of realizing Chinese socialism. This way, the recipients of our education will become the advocates and defenders of socialism with Chinese characteristics. At a ceremony marking the 95th Anniversary of the Founding of the Communist Party of China in 2016, Xi Jinping emphasized that the entire Party should be confident in our path, theory, system, and culture. He stated, "Of all the political parties, countries, and peoples in the world today, none have as much cause to be confident as the CPC, the People's Republic of China, and the Chinese people."[1] The education

---

1 Xi Jinping: "Speech at a Ceremony Marking the 95th Anniversary of the Founding of the Communist Party of China," *Qiushi Journal*, October-December 2016, p. 10.

sector needs to explain clearly the origin, evolution, and direction of socialism with Chinese characteristics, as well as its originality, values, and distinctive features, to help the people understand and recognize its strengths and enhance their confidence in it.

To ensure that education serves the consolidation and development of Chinese socialism, we must nurture a new generation of capable young people who are well prepared to join the socialist cause through education. From a historical and practical perspective, all countries and societies regard education as an important way to maintain political leadership and social stability. China is a socialist country led by the CPC. This requires education in China to take as its important mission the consolidation and development of socialism with Chinese characteristics while nurturing generations of capable talent. Such talent should support Party leadership and the Chinese socialist system, and they should devote themselves to developing and promoting this system. This is a matter of principle for educational development, for which there is no room for ambiguity.

To ensure that education serves the consolidation and development of Chinese socialism, we must fully leverage education to make Chinese socialism more mature and better established. To improve this system, we should promote practice-based institutional innovation with theoretical innovation. This requires the education sector to advance theoretical research on the innovation of Chinese socialism and to provide intellectual support to develop institutions and systems that are comprehensive, scientific, and effective. Similarly, we should explore and innovate socialist education system with Chinese characteristics to better consolidate and develop socialism with Chinese characteristics.

## 3.4 Education for serving reform and opening up, and socialist modernization

To have education serve reform and opening up, as well as socialist modernization, is an essential requirement for comprehensively deepening reform, promoting opening up, and building a great modern socialist country. Education develops itself by serving the country. The reform, opening up, and modernization have provided a broad stage for China's education and contributed to its rapid advancement. To realize the great rejuvenation of the Chinese nation in the new era, we must continue to deepen reform, open wider to the outside world, and accelerate socialist modernization. Educational development must adapt to the new circumstances and requirements of reform and opening up and socialist modernization in the new era. And to that end, serving reform and opening up and socialist modernization should be taken as an important task.

To have education serve reform and opening up and socialist modernization, we must train talent at all levels. Talented people are a strategic resource for realizing national rejuvenation and for gaining the initiative in international competition. To promote reform and opening up and socialist modernization in the new era, we must train and attract a large contingent of excellent talent to participate in the great endeavor of national rejuvenation. Thus, we must rely on education to nurture innovative personnel in the fields of science, technology, philosophy, and social sciences, as well as other professional spheres.

To have education serve reform and opening up and socialist modernization, the education sector must provide intellectual support. The increasingly arduous tasks of reform and development call for ever stronger intellectual support. Xi Jinping attaches great importance to the development of think tanks, requiring new types of think tanks with distinctive Chinese features that can facilitate science-based and democratic decision-making, modernize China's system and capacity for governance, and enhance its soft power. He has noted that priority should be given to the development of a contingent of high-caliber, specialized, and influential think tanks that are clearly positioned, well differentiated, right sized, and reasonably structured. The education sector must fully leverage its abundant human resources, complete academic disciplines, vibrant ideas, and strong foundations to serve the economy and people's wellbeing through more research and innovation and through more policy recommendations to decision makers.

# Chapter 5

China's Own Path of
Education

China's unique history, culture, and conditions determine that its affairs, education included, must be handled in accordance with its own features and realities. General Secretary Xi Jinping noted at the National Education Conference that to make our education successful, we must uphold socialism with Chinese characteristics while being grounded in our own culture and connected with the world, and serving the present and looking into the future, and that we must establish a modern education system up to international standard but with Chinese characteristics. These observations are implanted in our cultural foundations and embody a high degree of self-awareness and self-confidence. They will undoubtedly guide the Chinese socialist education onto a wider path.

# 1. Aligning Education with the Reality of China

"If we gain a firm foothold, we will be able to withstand any challenge." This quote vividly depicts Xi Jinping's view on education in China. When he was working in Zhejiang province, he assigned Zhejiang University as his work-related institution, which he visited 18 times. He encouraged Zhejiang University to proceed from China's specific situations, follow the direction of socialism, and explore a unique path to a world-class university with Chinese characteristics. In May 2014, at the meeting with teachers and students of Peking University, Xi further pointed out, "In this world, there cannot be a second Harvard, a second Oxford, a second Stanford, a second MIT, or a second Cambridge; but there can be one Peking University, one Tsinghua University, one Zhejiang University, one Fudan University, and one Nanjing University. We should draw on the best practices in running institutions of higher learning, follow the inherent laws of education, and foster more outstanding universities by grounding ourselves in our own culture."[1]

## 1.1 The path of education determined by national history, culture, and conditions

We must follow our own path in education since we have our unique history. The history of Chinese civilization, the struggle of the Chinese people since 1840, the journey of the Communist Party of

---

1 Xi Jinping: *Young People Should Practice the Core Socialist Values—Speech at the Meeting with Teachers and Students of Peking University*, Chinese edition, People's Publishing House, Beijing, 2014, p. 13.

China, the development of the People's Republic of China, and the reform and opening up are all interconnected. In a keynote speech at the College of Europe in Bruges, Belgium in 2014, Xi Jinping said, "One cannot understand China without understanding its history, culture, mentalities of the Chinese people, and the profound changes taking place in China today."[1] Compared with other countries, the history and culture of China are unique and complex. They represent the deepest spiritual pursuit of the Chinese nation, and have provided rich nourishments for the survival and thriving of the nation. The contemporary China is the continuation and development of the historical China, and its thought and culture have been inherited from the past and elevated to new levels. Likewise, we must draw nutrition and strength from our history and traditions in running education. Only in this way can we better develop education.

We must follow our own path in education because of our unique culture. Xi Jinping said, "Outstanding traditional culture is the root of the heritage and development of a country and a nation. Renouncing it is tantamount to severing our cultural lifeline."[2] Confidence in one's culture is the fundamental and lasting force driving the development of a nation. If a country or a nation does not cherish its own thought and culture, or worse, forsakes it, it will lose its soul and not be able to sustain itself. China's great tradition, created long ago and carried forward over thousands of years, is the root and soul of the nation. During the long course of history, the wise and courageous Chinese people have created a beautiful homeland through diligent work, a homeland in which all ethnic groups live together in harmony. They have developed dynamic culture, and unique values and philosophies. The great rejuvenation of the Chinese nation requires the support of a prosperous Chinese culture; likewise, successful education depends on a solid

---

1 Xi Jinping: *Speeches at the Third Nuclear Security Summit and During His Visits to Four European Countries, UNESCO Headquarters, and EU Headquarters*, Chinese edition, People's Publishing House, Beijing, 2014, p. 45.
2 Xi Jinping: *The Governance of China*, Vol. II, Foreign Languages Press, Beijing, 2017, p. 341.

cultural foundation. In reforming China's education, we should hold on to our cultural genes, and draw strength from the glorious history of the Chinese nation and the great achievements in national development; we should transform and innovate our culture, enhance our cultural confidence, and use our culture as the foundation for socialist education with Chinese characteristics in the new era.

We must follow our own path in education because of our unique national conditions. Xi Jinping remarked that the answers to China's questions can only be found in this country. Although Chinese socialism has entered a new era and the principal challenges in Chinese society have changed, the fact that our country is still and will long remain at the initial stage of socialism has not changed, and China's international status as the world's largest developing country has not changed. As we run socialist education, we should uphold the socialist direction and adopt a people-centered approach. In addition, because educational resources are not evenly distributed and there are still many shortfalls, we should develop the education system to the best of our ability, and bear in mind that we are still at the initial stage of socialism and we are operating the world's largest education system. The understanding of this context is key to well-rounded development and all-round social progress.

## 1.2 Bolstering confidence in education rooted in China

To rejuvenate our nation through education, we must foster confidence in education rooted in China. Only a confident people will flourish. Xi Jinping said that students should be inspired to foster the long-term goal of communism and the shared ideal of socialism with Chinese characteristics and that they should have confidence in the path, theory, system, and culture of Chinese socialism, and aspire to achieve national rejuvenation. The strategy of the CPC and the Chinese people—to develop the country through self-reliance and based on national conditions, and also by drawing on other cultures—is correct and must be upheld. Likewise, we should demonstrate cultural confidence when reforming our education by preserving good practices while making up for weaknesses. Do not forget we are running socialist education on our own land, where we can draw nourishment from our cultural heritage dating back thousands of years. We can benefit from CPC leadership, and count on people's support. These are the sources of our strength and confidence. China's education must take on the historic mission of national rejuvenation, and stay on the path of socialism with Chinese characteristics.

The profound educational philosophy of the Chinese nation is the source of our confidence in pursuing China-rooted education. Xi Jinping said, "Rooted in a land of more than 9.6 million square kilometers, nourished by a culture of more than 5,000 years, and blessed with the strength of more than 1.3 billion people, we have an infinitely vast stage of our era, a heritage of unmatched depth, and incomparable resolve that enable us to forge ahead on the road of socialism with Chinese characteristics."[1] The Chinese nation should have such confidence, and so should every Chinese. With its civilization spanning over 5,000 years, China has a rich cultural heritage, where we can find insightful educational concepts such as "learning being an endless journey," "education for all," and "individualized education." These have laid a solid foundation for China-rooted education. We should explore and promote traditional Chinese values such as benevolence, humanity, integrity, righteousness, harmony, and universal peace while carrying forward the revolutionary culture and developing a strong socialist culture. Patriotism, collectivism, and socialist education should be strengthened by various means so that people will adopt sound views on history, nations, countries, and culture while being proud to be Chinese. The path of socialist education will thus extend wider and wider.

The country's achievements in education since the founding of the People's Republic of China in 1949 are the foundation of our

---

1 Xi Jinping: "Secure a Decisive Victory in Building a Moderately Prosperous Society in All Respects and Strive for the Great Success of Socialism with Chinese Characteristics for a New Era—Report Delivered at the 19th National Congress of the Communist Party of China," *The Governance of China*, Vol. III, Foreign Languages Press, Beijing, 2020, p. 76.

confidence in China-rooted education. Over the past seven decades, the country's overall education is on a par with, or even exceeds, the global average. The quality of education has improved significantly, the conditions of education have undergone great changes, the international influence of our education has expanded considerably, and the education reform has deepened. Since the 18th CPC National Congress in 2012, in particular, China's education has developed comprehensively with more distinctive features. The pace of modernization has quickened, people's sense of gain has increased, and individual needs have been better met. As a result of its performance in education, China has become one of the ten "Champion Countries" designated by the United Nations for the Global Education First Initiative. Its achievements and basic experience have showcased the quality of its educational endeavors and highlighted the strengths of its system and political path. Nevertheless, China's education is still not devoid of problems, but we cannot solve them by merely copying the practices of other countries. Instead, we should ground ourselves in China, run education according to our own situation, and follow the inherent laws of education; we must constantly innovate and draw on the world's best practices. If this is done, the country's education will surely enjoy a better tomorrow.

## 2. Following the Path of Socialist Education with Chinese Characteristics

The path we take determines our future. If we take the wrong path, we will never reach our goal, no matter how attractive it is. The prosperity of socialist education with Chinese characteristics requires us to be grounded in China and connected with the world, and serve the present and look into the future; it also requires us to free our mind and innovate, keep up with the times, adapt the world's advanced experience to China's situation, and explore practices that meet our national conditions.

## 2.1 China-rooted and globally connected

China cannot develop in isolation from the rest of the world, nor can the world achieve prosperity without China. Xi Jinping has said, "We live in a time of openness and connectivity. History shows that openness leads to progress while seclusion leaves one behind. The world today is a global village, where our interests and our economic and social progress interconnect. To achieve common prosperity in today's world, we have no choice but to pursue greater connectivity and integration."[1] Over the past four decades, China's education has always been rooted in the Chinese soil and connected with the world. It has expanded in the process of international exchange and is exerting global influence.

---

### ✺ *Quote from Xi Jinping* ✺

We will strengthen people-to-people and cultural exchanges with other countries, giving prominence to Chinese culture while drawing on other cultures.

—Report to the 19th CPC National Congress, October 18, 2017

---

*Giving prominence to Chinese culture while drawing on other cultures.* We must draw on the achievements of other civilizations. However, we should not undervalue our own or blindly copy the models of other countries, and we will never accept their diktats. Likewise, in socialist education with Chinese characteristics, we should not simply repeat our own historical practices, nor should we replicate education models of other countries. Rather, we should make use of desirable foreign practices to reinforce the Chinese system. We should be pragmatic and critical in identifying approaches suited to China's conditions and supportive of socialist education.

---

1 Xi Jinping: *Openness for Greater Prosperity, Innovation for a Better Future—Keynote Speech at the Opening of the Boao Forum for Asia Annual Conference 2018*, Chinese edition, People's Publishing House, Beijing, 2018, pp. 6-7.

*China's education going global.* Xi Jinping has noted on multiple occasions the need to develop modern education with Chinese characteristics that meets international standard. According to him, we should make use of useful theories and academic achievements of human civilization; we should learn from international experience in education reform to improve the quality of education; and we should cultivate more and higher-caliber personnel, and provide opportunities for them to make good use of their talent. We must open still wider and strengthen interaction and friendship with other peoples. We hope that young people of all countries will see the world with appreciation, maintain the attitude of sharing and mutual learning, and work to promote exchanges and harmony between different cultures, thus contributing to the creation of a community with a shared future for humanity. Chinese students and scholars studying abroad should use the opportunity for more exchanges, acting as unofficial ambassadors for people-to-people friendship, telling China's stories well and having China's voice heard, so as to gain understanding and support of other countries. In education, we should expand international cooperation, promote ICT (information and communications technology) application, support developing countries, and ensure sustainable development.

## 2.2 Serving the present and looking into the future

Education reform and development should serve the needs of the times. The Chinese nation has made historic leaps from liberation to prosperity, and thence is becoming a stronger nation. But the successes of yesterday do not guarantee successes of tomorrow, and the glories of the past do not guarantee glories in the future. Xi Jinping has noted that the most important task of China today is to deliver on the Two Centenary Goals, and realize the Chinese Dream of national rejuvenation. As Chinese socialism has entered a new era, the principal challenges facing Chinese society have changed. Reform and opening up, socialist modernization, well-rounded human development, and all-round social progress—these have all laid down new and higher requirements for education reform and development. We are like examinees sitting the tests posted by this era, and the people will review our results. In education, we should keep in mind that in the new era of socialism with Chinese characteristics, the overriding goal is socialist modernization and national rejuvenation. We should keep improving our ability to meet the needs of the times and accomplish the great cause, and construct a moderately prosperous society in all respects and a great modern socialist country.

---

### ◎～*Quote from Xi Jinping*～◎

Education connects us with the past, forges the present, and creates the future; it is an important force driving forward human civilization.

—Congratulatory message for the launch of Schwarzman College, Tsinghua University, September 10, 2016

---

Education should be anchored to the future. Education concerns the future of the nation and each individual, and therefore long-term planning and top-level design are needed. In today's world of rapid technological progress, modernization, and population growth, we must counter global challenges and support sustainable development with science and technology. Looking ahead, we should focus on technological frontiers. We should foster a large contingent of world-class scientists and technologists in strategically important fields, scientific and technological leaders, and young scientists and engineers, as well as high-performing innovation teams, so as to make major breakthroughs in pioneering basic research and groundbreaking original innovations. Meanwhile, we should make education modernization future-oriented and supportive of the nation's modernization. We must put in place a long-term mechanism to modernize the state governance system and capacity, and build a new paradigm in which the whole society participates in the development and governance of education, and everyone enjoys the fruits of education progress.

Educational development should balance the needs of the present and the future. In his congratulatory message for the launch of the Schwarzman College at Tsinghua University, General Secretary Xi Jinping noted that education connects us with the past, forges the present, and creates the future, and it is an important force driving forward human civilization. Only by looking back at the road we have traveled, comparing it with others' roads, and then looking ahead, can we figure out where we came from and where we are going, and gain insights into many issues. The new era we live in is not only the best of times for the Chinese nation since 1840, but also the most critical time for the rejuvenation of the Chinese nation. We should remember our own culture, take nutrition from other cultures, and look ahead. We should not only look inward, studying issues of China, but also look outward, studying issues of humanity. We should look ahead, assessing the trend of socialism with Chinese characteristics, and look back, passing on traditional Chinese culture. We should cultivate more talent to meet the needs of the Party, the country, the people, and the times.

## 3. Establishing a Modern Education System with Chinese Characteristics and Up to International Standard

What is unique for a nation is precious for the world. China's education is expected to have Chinese characteristics and follow the path of socialism. Meanwhile, we should adopt a global vision and the best practices in running schools. Xi Jinping has noted that educators should recognize their mission and responsibility, contribute to modernizing education in accordance with international standard, and nurture new generations for the socialist cause. *China's Education Modernization 2035* highlights the major problems of the country's education. Future-oriented, it sets ten strategic tasks for modernization:

- Promoting Xi Jinping Thought on Socialism with Chinese Characteristics for a New Era;
- Developing world-class education with Chinese characteristics;
- Promoting equal access to quality education at all levels;
- Achieving universal and equal access to basic public education services;
- Building lifelong learning systems for all;
- Fostering high-caliber talent for innovation;
- Nurturing high-caliber, specialized, and innovative teachers;
- Accelerating ICT-based education reform;
- Opening up education to the outside world; and
- Modernizing the education governance system and capacity.

## 3.1 Promoting high-quality education at all levels

*Providing successful basic education.* Xi Jinping has noted that basic education is a fundamental and leading part of the national education system. This point must be clearly understood. We must fully implement the Party's education policy and improve our basic education through multiple measures. Basic education fosters virtues. The teaching of morality, ethics, and core socialist values should be reinforced in order to help students develop a strong sense of self-esteem, self-confidence, self-reliance, and self-improvement. As basic education is the foundation in national education, we should make the foundation solid and follow the way adolescents grow. Basic education should be guided by a correct understanding of human development and thus contribute to well-rounded human development. Schools and teachers should be encouraged to foster their unique strengths. Basic education embraces the common endeavor of the whole society and requires close cooperation among schools, families, and society. The state needs to increase support for basic education, strengthen pre-school education, equalize participation in the nine-year compulsory education, and make available senior high school education to all adolescents. We should optimize the allocation of educational resources, and narrow the gaps between regions, between urban and rural areas, and between schools.

*Achieving intensive growth of higher education.* Higher education is crucial to the country's development and the future of the nation. China's university enrolments and the number of graduates each year rank first in the world, but quantitative growth does not necessarily mean qualitative improvement. Therefore, improving the quality is a must for success in higher education. We must ensure that higher education supports economic and social development. We must develop world-class higher education institutions to ensure that each becomes distinctive in its own area. We must formulate policies for the classification and development of higher education institutions to help universities position themselves and pursue differentiated development. We must promote the transformation of undergraduate institutions at different localities while optimizing the structure of talent cultivation and helping higher education institutions restructure their disciplines and majors through national enrolment planning, employment feedback, funding, standard setting, and evaluation. We must strengthen the cultivation of innovative personnel, especially top-notch talent, and increase the supply of innovative, interdisciplinary, and professional personnel with practical skills. We must strengthen the innovation system in higher education institutions, build world-class national innovation bases, and enhance applied basic research, thus improving the innovation capacity of higher education institutions.

*Building a technical and vocational education system with Chinese characteristics.* Technical and vocational education is an important part of the national education system and in human resources development, and a major path for some young people to live a fruitful life. Technical and vocational education shoulders the responsibilities of developing a diverse pool of talent, passing on technical skills, and boosting employment and entrepreneurship. Therefore, it should be given high priority and developed at a faster pace. A correct understanding of success should be developed in society. We should realize that creative work, skilled work, and manual work are equally great, valuable, and glorious. Education should contribute to social progress and employment. We should extend institutional reform, optimize the structure of technical and vocational education, connect it with industrial needs, encourage partnerships between schools and enterprises, and connect study with work and knowledge with action. We should build a number of high-level technical and vocational colleges and disciplines, create innovative technical and vocational education models, and guide society, especially industries and enterprises, in support of technical and vocational education. We should allocate more resources to technical and vocational education in poor and rural areas and areas with large ethnic populations and build a strong technical and vocational education system with Chinese characteristics.

*Building a lifelong education system that serves all people.* As lifestyle and work patterns constantly change, lifelong learning has become an important concept in modern education. Xi Jinping has noted that we should build a digitalized, personalized, and lifelong education network that allows anyone to learn anywhere and anytime, and make sure that education institutions observe the inherent laws of education, talent cultivation, and well-rounded development. Besides providing quality basic education, higher education, and technical and vocational education, we need to enhance family education, special education, continuing education, and community-based education. We should standardize compulsory education and build boarding schools in areas with large ethnic populations, offer free secondary technical and vocational education, and improve higher education and bilingual[1] education there.

## 3.2 Developing world-class universities and first-class disciplines

The quality of higher education is an important indicator of a country's development status and potential. Xi Jinping has said, "The CPC Central Committee has resolved to build world-class universities and disciplines, which means scaling up China's higher education and core

---

1 The two languages concerned are Putonghua (Mandarin Chinese) and the local ethnic language.

competitiveness."[1] The Party and the government are witnessing a crucial stage, so never before have we had such a pressing need for higher education, and never before have we had so much demand for knowledge and talent. China's higher education should deliver a large number of people with integrity and skills—people who can contribute to realizing the Two Centenary Goals and the great national rejuvenation. We must build a number of high-level socialist universities with Chinese characteristics that can be leaders and models of higher education in China, and raise some of them and their disciplines to world-class ranking to increase the overall strength of China's higher education and its international competitiveness in producing outstanding talent and research results.

─ ◎ *Quote from Xi Jinping* ◎ ──────────

World-class Chinese universities must have distinctive Chinese characteristics. We will not be successful if we simply follow others and copy what they are doing.

—Speech at the meeting with teachers and students of Peking University, May 4, 2014

World-class universities in China must have Chinese characteristics. Xi Jinping has emphasized that a first-class university is recognized for its distinctive characteristics; we will not be successful if we simply follow others and copy what they are doing. The success of a university lies in its reputation, its heritage, and its achievements. It takes a long time for a university to build its reputation. There are many international and domestic rankings of universities; we can refer to them, but we should not rely on them too much. It is impossible to evaluate a university by reference to no more than a few statistics. We should transform our confidence in the path, theory, system, and culture of socialism with Chinese characteristics into confidence in building world-class universities.

────────────

1 Xi Jinping: *The Governance of China*, Vol. II, Foreign Languages Press, Beijing, 2017, p. 406.

Successful higher education and world-class universities are evaluated by their ability to produce qualified people. Xi Jinping said at the National Conference on Moral and Political Work in Institutions of Higher Learning that only those universities that provide society with outstanding brains can be considered world-class ones. In 2018, he further noted at the meeting with teachers and students of Peking University that as long as we can train capable people well prepared for the socialist cause, our universities will have a place and a voice in the world. In developing modern, world-class education with Chinese characteristics, we should regard achievements in moral education as the fundamental criterion for all the work of a university. Moral education should be internalized into all areas and aspects of university management and given first priority. We should build an education system in which students' moral, intellectual, physical, and aesthetic development is all fostered with a love for labor; we also need a sound evaluation system to ensure the fundamental task of moral education is performed, thus turning the strengths of Chinese socialism into an ability to train capable people—people who are both socialism-minded and professionally competent to meet the needs of the Party, the state, the people, and the times. We should build world-class universities and disciplines with Chinese characteristics that prioritize moral education, support the innovation-driven development strategy, and serve our economic and social development. In this way, we will increase the comprehensive strength and international competitiveness of China's higher education, and realize the Two Centenary Goals and the Chinese Dream of national rejuvenation.

## 3.3 Upgrading the talent cultivation system

"He who digs a well starts with a three-inch pit and eventually makes it into a well that is ten thousand feet deep."[1] What students should and can learn, and how well they learn are determined by the

---

1 Cited from *Liuzi* by Liu Zhou (514–565), who was a man of letters of the State of Northern Qi (550–577) during the Northern and Southern dynasties (420–589).

system's ability to foster talent. Xi Jinping said at the National Education Conference that we need to build an education system which fosters students' moral, intellectual, physical, and aesthetic development and a love for labor, and we need to raise the country's ability to foster talent. The cultivation of character should be integrated into all aspects of education—moral, intellectual, and social practice, and at all levels—basic, technical and vocational, and higher education. Academic disciplines, didactics, course materials, and school management should all be geared to this purpose. Teachers and students should have this goal in mind.

*Creating academic disciplines with Chinese characteristics.* Xi Jinping has noted that efforts should be made to form cross-disciplinary clusters and strong research teams, and to enhance collaborative innovation across disciplines and the support for original, systematic, and leading research. We should optimize regional distribution, discipline structure, and academic programs of universities, establish a mechanism for adjusting academic disciplines and programs, and cultivate innovative, interdisciplinary, and application-oriented talent. The development of a country depends not only on natural sciences but also on philosophy and social sciences. To develop Chinese socialism, we must give priority to philosophy and social sciences. A country with distinctive features of philosophy and social sciences is sophisticated, strong, and self-confident. In philosophy and social sciences, China ranks high in the number of researchers and publications and in government input. However, our capacity to raise academic questions, produce ideas, set standards, and lead academic discourse in international academia is not commensurate with our overall national strength and international status. To solve this problem, we must be grounded in Chinese conditions in developing philosophy and social sciences, introduce thoughts from other countries, use history to serve the present, and focus on the future of humanity. We must make these disciplines unique, so that they can display Chinese characteristics in guiding principles, and disciplinary, academic, and discourse systems.

*Improving teaching systems.* Xi Jinping has said that with the development of information technology, the ways of acquiring and imparting knowledge and the relationship between teaching and learning have undergone revolutionary changes. We should study the means of fostering talent, update teaching philosophy, and optimize the content of teaching; we should also improve teaching methods, enhance teaching support systems, and focus on key areas, in order to build a high-level teaching system and improve the quality of teaching. We must attach importance to developing the teaching system for philosophy and social sciences, and make sure that Xi Jinping Thought on Socialism with Chinese Characteristics for a New Era is included in textbooks and classroom teaching and understood by students. In this regard, schools should perform a major function. We must increase the weight of classroom teaching in teachers' performance evaluation and encourage them to devote more energy to teaching. We should encourage them to take teaching as their most important work, and make the best use of the classroom, the campus, and their scholarship and experience to inspire students to pursue the true, the good, and the beautiful. We should address such issues as why to teach, what to teach, whom to teach, and how to teach. We must incorporate Xi Jinping Thought on Socialism with Chinese Characteristics for a New Era into the whole process of teaching and research, and translate it into political conviction, theoretical awareness, and scientific thinking.

*Doing a good job in course materials development.* Course materials are the main vehicle for disseminating knowledge. They reflect the values of a nation as an important tool of teaching and learning. Course materials must be guided by Marxism and its adaptation to the Chinese context; they must reflect the national spirit and values, the Party's education policy, and the cultural achievements and innovation outcomes of humanity. Xi Jinping has said, "Academic disciplines are inseparable from teaching materials, which cannot be developed systematically if the academic disciplines are not systematic. Conversely, without systematic development of teaching materials, academic disciplines will lose support and cannot sustain."[1] To foster talent, we must have good

---

1 Xi Jinping: *Speech at the Meeting on Philosophy and Social Sciences*, Chinese edition, People's Publishing House, Beijing, 2016, p. 23.

course materials, which must be developed from the perspective of cultivating new generations of socialist builders and ensuring a correct political orientation and values. Mechanisms and institutional innovations should be introduced in the compilation, distribution, and application of course materials; the curricula of elementary and secondary schools and universities should be well designed; curriculum standards should be developed by category; and information technology should be adopted to enrich and innovate teaching methods. We should improve the national textbook compilation system through unified administration, delegation of authority, and guidance by category. Course materials should be politically reliable, scientifically sound, up-to-date, systematic, and with Chinese characteristics. We should improve the mechanisms for textbook compilation, review, selection, and removal, forming a system that meets the requirements of socialist development, reflects the latest academic achievements, and covers all subject areas.

---

### ⊚~*Quote from Xi Jinping*~⊚

Talent cultivation involves the systems of academic disciplines, teaching, textbooks, and management, with moral and political education running through all of them.

—Speech at the meeting with teachers and students of Peking University, May 2, 2018

---

*Improving the school management system.* We should reform the educational service supply system and education management to stimulate the vitality of education. In order to modernize the education governance system and enhance the governing capacity, we should extend reform in the internal, personnel, remuneration, and teaching management of schools through reforms in educational service supply, education management, funding mechanisms, examination, enrolment, and employment systems. We should improve the law-based management of education. A complete system of educational laws and regulations should be enacted to improve the legal support for school operations. We should improve the implementation of laws and enhance compliance supervision while improving the structure and systems of education by increasing the number of education inspectors who perform multiple functions: administrative and academic supervision, and evaluation and monitoring. We must make better use of inspection results and improve the authority and effectiveness of inspection. We must improve schools' capacity for self-management, improve their governance structure, and facilitate the adoption of university charters. We should encourage private schools to establish a modern school system based on their for-profit or not-for-profit status. We should promote the regular participation of society in education governance by establishing a system of social participation in school management, evaluation, and supervision.

*Strengthening the moral and political education system.* Xi Jinping has said, "Talent cultivation involves the academic discipline system, the teaching system, the textbook system, and the management system, with moral and political education running through all of them."[1] Moral and political education plays a key role in raising China's system for fostering talent to a higher level. Education in morality is the lifeline of all school work; it should be done on a daily basis and reach into the hearts of people. We should carry out the Party's education policy in full, follow the inherent laws of education, and take building strong moral character as the central task. In moral and political education, we must make sure that all faculty and staff are involved, and all activities are aimed at this purpose. We should imbue students with ideals, beliefs, and core socialist values, and equip them with Marxist theory throughout the process of education—in moral and political classes, in other courses, and in the work of all educators. In other words, moral and political education should go hand in hand with disciplinary studies for the purpose of students' whole-person development.

---

1 Xi Jinping: *Speech at the Meeting with Teachers and Students of Peking University*, Chinese edition, People's Publishing House, Beijing, 2018, p. 10.

# Chapter 6

Education for the People

We should remain true to our original aspiration and keep our mission in mind. The original aspiration and mission of the Chinese communists is to seek happiness for the Chinese people and the rejuvenation of the Chinese nation. We aim to fulfil the people's desire for a better life. Our people have an ardent love for life and look forward to better education. At the National Education Conference in 2018, General Secretary Xi Jinping proposed a people-centered development agenda. This proposal, reflecting the CPC's fundamental purpose of wholeheartedly serving the people and the Party's deep concern for them, is the starting point for the reform and development of China's education, as well as the guiding principle for making education satisfactory to the people.

# 1.  Staying True to People-Centered Education

In March 2019, when President Xi Jinping was visiting Rome, Roberto Fico, President of the Italian Chamber of Deputies, asked him how he felt when he was elected President of China. Xi said it was a great responsibility and an arduous task to run a country as large as China. "Selfless shall I be for the good of my people. I would like to devote myself to serving the Chinese people and the nation's development." In just a few words, he fully expressed his loyalty to his own country and people, his dedication to serving the people, and his concern for and commitment to his country and people as a servant of the people.

The people are the real heroes. Their contribution determines the future of the CPC and China. Xi Jinping has repeatedly called for a people-centered approach to development, with commitment to the principle of development of the people, by the people, and for the people. In education, we should stay true to the value system that puts the people first, and constantly meet people's expectations for better education, so that all the people can share the benefits of educational development through participation. This way, they can contribute to society while developing themselves.

## 1.1 Meeting people's expectations for better education

Benefiting the people is the fundamental principle of governance. As the foundation of people's wellbeing, education involves every family and benefits all generations to come. It is, therefore, a major concern of the public. In November 2012, at the press conference by members of the Standing Committee of the Political Bureau of the 18th CPC Central Committee, Xi Jinping said, "Our people have an ardent love for life. They want to have better education, more stable jobs, more income, reliable social security, better medical and health care, improved housing conditions and a beautiful environment. They hope that their children will have sound growth, good jobs and more enjoyable lives."[1] These remarks manifest the CPC's principle of putting people first and its goal of socialist education with Chinese characteristics.

---

### ⊙～Quote from Xi Jinping～⊙

Equity in education is an important basis for social justice. We must enable all our people to share fully and fairly the benefits of educational development, and ensure education equity to enhance social justice.

—Speech during his visit to Beijing Bayi School, September 9, 2016

---

Education should be run in the fundamental interests of all the people. Meeting people's expectations and satisfying their needs is the starting point and ultimate goal of educational development. While reforming and developing education, we must approach problems and make decisions by siding with the people, striking a balance between the demands of people's immediate, long-term, and fundamental interests, and between individual and social needs. In a socialist country, where the people are the masters, the needs of the state and the people are inherently consistent. It is the fundamental interests of the country and the fundamental expectation of the people to cultivate talent through better and fairer education, to improve the overall caliber of the nation, to make it prosperous, and ultimately to achieve the great rejuvenation of the Chinese nation. The report to the 19th CPC National

---

1 Xi Jinping: *The Governance of China*, Vol. I, Foreign Languages Press, Beijing, 2018, p. 4.

Congress said, "Strengthening education is fundamental to our pursuit of national rejuvenation. We must give priority to education, further reform in education, speed up its modernization, and develop education that people are satisfied with."[1] The proposal highlights the social significance of turning China into an educational powerhouse as well as the basic requirements for a satisfactory education, thus reflecting the inherent unity of socialist education serving the people and socialist modernization.

We should address the most pressing and most immediate education issues that concern the people the most. The principal challenge facing Chinese society is unbalanced and inadequate development in the context of the people's ever-growing desire for a better life. Education is part of the fabric of society, and therefore part of this challenge. Xi Jinping has repeatedly said that China's educational development still witnesses regional, urban-rural, and inter-school gaps, and many weaknesses. In view of the new situations and problems in education, the state should guard against risks, highlight priorities, improve the system, and inform expectations. We should start with the biggest concerns and address the key, hotspot, and difficult issues that the public care about, so as to respond to people's expectations for better and fairer education.

## 1.2 Securing a greater sense of gain in education for the people

We should ensure that the underlying goal of socialism is that the general public share the fruits of education reform and development. People's wellbeing constitutes the foundation of happiness and social harmony. Education, an important means of improving the wellbeing of the people, needs to address the important issues of whom we are working for, and who will benefit. The people are

---

1 Xi Jinping: "Secure a Decisive Victory in Building a Moderately Prosperous Society in All Respects and Strive for the Great Success of Socialism with Chinese Characteristics for a New Era—Report Delivered at the 19th National Congress of the Communist Party of China," *The Governance of China*, Vol. III, Foreign Languages Press, Beijing, 2020, p. 48.

the principal players in society and the fundamental force behind social development. A people-centered approach to education will ensure that all people have a greater sense of gain in education, and enable them to move steadily toward well-rounded development and common prosperity. Xi Jinping, at the second full assembly of the Fifth Plenary Session of the 18th CPC Central Committee, said, "[O]ur driving principle must be that development is for the people and by the people, and its benefits are shared by the people."[1] Letting people share the fruits of reform and development is the essence of socialism. It demonstrates the superiority of socialism and the CPC's whole-heartedness in serving the people. Since the founding of the People's Republic of China, the CPC and the government have attached great importance to developing education. The country has built the world's largest education system, guaranteeing the right to education for hundreds of millions of people, and having improved the education level of the entire nation, and promoted economic and social development. Since the 18th CPC National Congress, policies and measures for equal access to education have taken root, basic public services in education are being steadily equalized, and visible progress has been made in China's education reform, development, and modernization. As the CPC continues its commitment to the people-centered philosophy of development and comprehensively implements its education policy in the interests of the people, the general public have a greater sense of gain in education.

The unremitting efforts made by the CPC and the government to enhance people's sense of gain in education reflect the people-centered value system in developing education. Since the 18th CPC National Congress, the CPC and the government have endeavored to score high on the "exam paper" of running education to meet people's expectations and respond to their interests and concerns, promoting equal access to education, improving the quality of education, thus providing tangible benefits to the general public. Education at all levels and

---

1 Xi Jinping: *The Governance of China*, Vol. II, Foreign Languages Press, Beijing, 2017, p. 220.

of all types is accelerating; socialist education with Chinese characteristics benefiting all the people is taking shape; online, community-based, and senior citizen education are flourishing; and a learning society, where everyone learns and may learn anywhere and anytime, is materializing. People's dream of having access to better and fairer education is becoming a reality, and they have a greater sense of educational gain.

To guarantee people's sense of gain in education, it is important to respond to public opinion and to put it into practice. Xi Jinping has said, "The people-centered development philosophy is not an abstract, abstruse concept. We will not restrict ourselves to lip service or idle reflection, but put it into practice in all areas of social and economic development."[1] The country continues to promote equal access to education, helping individuals achieve self-development through education and poor areas get out of poverty, increasing upward social mobility, and enhancing people's sense of gain in education. We should coordinate and balance the distribution of educational resources and improve the conditions of disadvantaged compulsory education schools in poverty-stricken areas to close the urban-rural education gap. We should implement special national programs on enrolling students from rural and poverty-stricken areas to narrow regional education gaps, and implement the Program on Rejuvenating Higher Education in Central and Western Regions and the Collaboration Program on Supporting Enrolment in Central and Western Regions to accelerate the development of education for ethnic minorities and narrow inter-school gaps. We should improve the overall level of ethnic education, heighten public awareness of ethnic solidarity and progress, build a strong sense of community among the Chinese people, and help different ethnic groups remain closely united and work jointly for common prosperity and development. We should keep improving the financial aid system for students at all levels and of all types of education, remit tuition and miscellaneous fees for officially registered low-income students in

---

1 Xi Jinping: *The Governance of China*, Vol. II, Foreign Languages Press, Beijing, 2017, p. 235.

public senior high schools, create more educational opportunities for people with disabilities, provide better guarantee of education for relocated children of migrant workers and support services for left-behind children in rural areas, and narrow the education gaps between different groups. All these measures, a reflection of the people-centered philosophy of educational development, ensure that all people have a real sense of gain in education.

## 2. Equitably Sharing Educational Benefits

The key to the people-centered approach to education lies in optimized allocation of educational resources and narrowed education gaps through more effective institutional arrangements. We should develop education for all and lifelong education, and accelerate progress toward a learning society while making the education "cake" bigger and cutting it fairer, so that everyone has an equitable share of educational development.

### 2.1 Optimizing the allocation of educational resources and closing education gaps

We should optimize the allocation of educational resources, expand the coverage of basic public services in education, and improve the quality and standard of education. Basic public services in education are some of the immediate issues that concern the people the most, and are the prerequisite for good health and contentment of the people and their social integration. To meet people's basic needs and ensure that they are able to enter the moderately prosperous society together, we must improve basic public services in education. To narrow the education gaps, we must manage the governance better, promote structural reforms in education, and proactively adapt to economic and social development and the needs of the people. We should unleash the vitality of the system, make breakthroughs, take the initiative, optimize the allocation of resources, revitalize the education system, preserve the basics, narrow development gaps, and promote equity. More public educational resources should be allocated to less developed regions and schools, weak links, and people in need, thus contributing to coordinated development across regions and between urban and rural areas.

---

### ⚬♦ *Quote from Xi Jinping* ✦⚬

Through ICT-enabled education, we will gradually narrow the digital divide across regions and between urban and rural areas, and promote education equity, so that hundreds of millions of children may share quality education under the same sky and change their destiny through knowledge.

—Congratulatory letter to the International Conference on ICT and Post-2015 Education, May 22, 2015

---

We should attach great importance to compulsory education in rural areas and coordinate development across urban and rural areas. Compulsory education is a national undertaking of public welfare and a basic public service that must be developed as a priority. The Fifth Plenary Session of the 18th CPC Central Committee proposed to improve the institutions and mechanisms for integrating urban and rural development, and ensure equal exchange of production factors, balanced allocation of public resources, and equal access to basic public services between urban and rural areas. To secure a decisive victory in building a moderately prosperous society in all respects, the 19th CPC National Congress proposed the rural revitalization strategy. To fully implement the strategy, we should develop balanced regional, urban-rural, and inter-school education, coordinate urban and rural compulsory education, and integrate school distribution with the rural revitalization strategy. In light of the requirement for building a moderately prosperous society in all respects, we should rationally balance compulsory education schools in urban and rural areas, guarantee the funding of compulsory education, coordinate the allocation of educational resources, and provide compulsory education for all permanent urban residents. *China's Education Modernization 2035* outlines the strategic tasks to ensure equal access to basic public education services, including equal access to compulsory education, the establishment of a long-term mechanism for school standardization, and the integration of the development of urban and rural compulsory education. After we have achieved county-wide balance in compulsory education, we should work on the balanced allocation of quality educational resources, ensure equal access to education at local schools for the children of migrant workers, create more places in urban schools, and improve the college entrance exam system so that children of migrant workers may take the exams where they currently reside. This will lay a solid foundation for the modernization of education and for building a moderately prosperous society in all respects.

We should promote education informatization and have quality educational resources shared. Running the largest education system in the world, China still faces the pressing problems of insufficient supply and unbalanced allocation of quality educational resources and there are practical barriers in sharing these resources among all people. Education informatization is able to break down barriers of time and space, contributing to rapid replication and dissemination via multiple presentation modes. It is therefore an effective means to ensure equal access to education and improve quality. Modernization supported and guided by informatization is a strategic choice for the reform and development of China's education in the new era. In the context of informatization, we should share quality resources, digital resources, high-caliber teachers, data, and digital dividends, carry out inter-school online teaching, build digital campuses, achieve balanced allocation of regional resources through Internet Plus, narrow the gaps in resources between urban and rural areas, different regions, and different schools, and close the digital divide. *China's Education Modernization 2035* proposes accelerating education reforms in the information age, building smart campuses, creating smart and integrated teaching, management, and service platforms, accelerating the reform of talent training by leveraging modern technologies, and achieving both mass education and personalized cultivation.

## 2.2 Striving for educational development in less developed and poor areas

During the annual meetings of China's top legislature and its top political advisory body in 2017, Xi Jinping expressed his concern about the "Cliff Village" in Liangshan Yi autonomous prefecture, Sichuan province. According to media coverage of the village in 2016, the only access from the village to the outside world, for children and adults alike, consisted of slippery rattan ladders. Xi read the reports with a heavy heart. He was relieved to hear about the construction of new steel staircases. In early 2018, a five-story teaching building was built for the local elementary school, and a pre-school education center established there. The parents no longer have to worry about their children's trips to and from school. The changes in the "Cliff Village" are a result of the efforts of the CPC and the government in developing education in the country's central and western regions. Since the 18th CPC National Congress, the country has taken major steps to elevate education in the central and western regions to a new level.

Accelerating the development of education in less developed regions and comprehensively upgrading education in the central and western regions are important measures for narrowing the education gaps and building a moderately prosperous society in all respects. Xi Jinping has said that we should double our efforts to coordinate urban and rural and regional development, increase support for less developed and rural areas, gradually narrow the urban-rural gap in development, and achieve common prosperity. The underdeveloped areas in China are mostly in the central and western regions, where education is much less developed than that in coastal provinces. Due to natural, historical, and social reasons, their economy and society are lagging behind, with a poor educational foundation and weak support, especially in rural, remote, poverty-stricken, and ethnic minority areas. In those places, high-caliber teachers are in short supply and teaching conditions are inadequate, resulting in generally low quality of education. This makes it difficult to meet the needs of the people there for a good education and for fostering talent for local development. In order to speed up the development of education in these areas, we should identify problems and fill the gaps. We should comprehensively improve education there so as to cultivate more talent who are willing to stay and contribute to local social and economic progress and to narrowing the gap between these areas and the eastern region.

We should overcome the weaknesses in the development of poor areas and take poverty alleviation through education as a permanent solution to the problem. Eliminating poverty, improving living standards, and achieving common prosperity are the basic requirements of socialism and an important mission of the CPC. In building a moderately prosperous society in all respects, poor areas are the weak links, and education in those areas is the weakest. Development-driven poverty alleviation depends on education. When working in Ningde, Fujian province (1988-1990), Xi Jinping thought about the relationship between poverty and education and between poverty and ignorance. He once said, "It is more difficult to develop education in poor areas, but it is those very areas that need education the most; the less education is developed there, the poorer they become."[1] Education in poor areas is a long-term project that must be implemented with great efforts. CPC committees and governments at all levels should give priority to education. Enabling children in poor areas to receive a good education is not only an important task in poverty alleviation and development, but also an important way of eradicating poverty and preventing it being passed down from one generation to another. Poverty alleviation is aimed not only at improving the level of education, but also at encouraging morale. We must increase government aid for basic education in old revolutionary

---

1  Xi Jinping: *Up and Out of Poverty*, Foreign Languages Press, Beijing, 2016, p. 180.

base areas, areas mainly populated by ethnic minorities, and remote and poverty-stricken areas. In particular, we should earmark funds for schools in poverty-stricken areas and improve the financial aid system for students from poor families. We will help children from poor families to gain access to education, and give all children confidence and hope that they need to create a bright future.

We should take targeted measures to reduce poverty through education and develop education in poor areas by making full use of local strengths. A targeted approach will determine whether the poverty alleviation drive is successful or not. The key to achieving tangible results in poverty alleviation is to find the right approaches, establish effective mechanisms, engage in targeted policy-making, and deliver real results in implementation. In November 2015, at the Central Conference on Poverty Alleviation and Development, Xi Jinping proposed that improving education in poverty-stricken areas should be one of the five measures to implement poverty relief.[1] He put forward new expectations and requirements for poverty alleviation through education. These include identifying roots of poverty, making targeted policies, reaching those in real need, and delivering genuine outcomes. These also include accurately locating the targets, allocating educational resources, and implementing measures. During the critical phase of the fight against poverty, we should give priority to technical and vocational education and training. If a child from a poor family can receive technical or vocational education, acquire a skill, and find a job, the family is likely to get out of poverty. Employment is related to people's wellbeing: if a person is employed, his entire family can be lifted out of poverty. We should develop education in poor areas by making full use of local strengths and providing specific and targeted guidance. We should increase

---

1 On October 16, 2015, at the Global Poverty Reduction and Development Forum, President Xi Jinping introduced five key measures to lift people out of poverty for the first time: some through increasing production, some through relocation, some through ecological compensation, some through education, and some through allowances to assist them in meeting their basic needs.

support for technical and vocational education in rural and poor areas, areas with large ethnic populations, while creating opportunities so that everyone may excel. We should take extraordinary policy initiatives for targeted poverty alleviation through education, target the weakest areas of education and the most disadvantaged groups, and achieve the goal that everyone attends school and learns skills, every family has hopes, and every county is supported. Having acquired knowledge and skills, our people will be more employable, feel more secure, and become better off. We will not let the children from poor families fail at the starting line, but ensure that they can enjoy a good education and have equal opportunities to realize their dreams.

## 2.3 Promoting lifelong education for all to build a learning society

In September 2013, in his message to the first anniversary of the UN Global Education First Initiative, President Xi Jinping said that China will promote education for all and lifelong education to build a learning society. Moreover, the country will work hard to ensure that every child has the opportunity to go to school, and to enable its 1.3 billion people to enjoy better and fairer education.

We should promote education for all and ensure that all people better enjoy their right to education. Since the 1990s, the Party and the government have always given priority to the strategic development of education, while promoting the nine-year universal compulsory education and the campaign to eradicate illiteracy among the young and the middle-aged, and developing rural education. As a result, the education level and quality of the population have been further enhanced. Since the 18th CPC National Congress, the Central Committee with General Secretary Xi Jinping at the core has given priority to developing education as a means of advancing the endeavors of the Party and the state in all areas, and has made achievements in education for all: government expenditure on education has been maintained at over 4% of China's GDP; the attendance rate for nine-year compulsory education has surpassed the average level of high-income countries; and the gross admission rates of senior high schools and higher education have risen. Although almost every Chinese may attend school, people's demand for quality educational resources has yet to be met, and "attending a good school" has become their new goal. As socialism with Chinese characteristics has entered a new era, China is shifting from a country that stresses quantity in education to one truly strong in education. We must promote education for all, improve the quality of education, and deliver quality education to meet the people's expectations, and ensure that they have access to better education.

We should improve continuing education to meet the diverse educational needs of the people. As a result of more than four decades of reform and opening up, China's productive forces have significantly improved. Naturally, people are expecting a better education and a better life. Continuing education constitutes an important part of people's diversified and multi-level needs for a more fulfilling life, and a strategic choice for their well-rounded development. The Party and the government are trying to make good education available to all and to improve education quality of the entire nation. Xi Jinping has reiterated the need to accelerate the building of a learning society and to promote well-rounded human development. To run quality continuing education, we should input more and improve the inclusiveness, flexibility, and adaptability of the education system. Reform in degree programs of continuing education should be oriented toward broadening knowledge, improving ability, and enriching life, while non-degree programs should aim to provide education and training for special groups of people, including workers, community residents, migrant workers in urban areas, modern farmers, and ex-servicemen. We should accelerate the development of education for senior citizens, coordinate the development of urban and rural community-based education, and build learning cities and organizations.

We should build a comprehensive lifelong learning system to enable a learning society. Well-rounded human development is a goal of socialism, and the well-rounded development of all people is a necessary component in building a moderately prosperous society in all respects. The new situation in the new era, reform and opening up, socialist modernization, and the promotion of well-rounded human development and all-round social progress all pose new and higher requirements for education and learning. With today's rapid scientific and technological progress, everyone must keep learning. Xi Jinping has said that we should take study as a pursuit, an interest, and a healthy lifestyle, so that we will engage in proactive and lifelong learning. We should link all types and levels of education, recognize different learning outcomes, coordinate all kinds of education, and promote the public sharing of learning resources. We should run quality open universities and develop online and distance education, for which we should expand the channels, and build a networked, digitalized, and personalized system for continuing education and lifelong learning. We should build a learning society, where anyone can learn anywhere and anytime. In this way, we will turn China into a powerhouse in terms of education, human resources, and talent.

## 3. Social Equity and Justice Through Equal Access to Education

"To govern the country, we should prioritize equality; with equality, peace will prevail under heaven."[1] Social equity and justice are common ideals, which a socialist society provides opportunities to realize. Equal access to education is an important foundation for social equity and justice. We should provide fair and quality education, improve the education level of all the people, and provide everyone with the opportunity to excel.

---

1 Cited from *Lü's Spring and Autumn Annals*, a collection of essays compiled by Lü Buwei (?-235 BC) in the late Warring States Period (475-221 BC).

### 3.1 The cornerstone of social equity: equal access to education

In September 2016, Xi Jinping said during a visit to Beijing Bayi School that equal access to education is the basis of social equity. His remarks indicate the connection between equal access to education and social equity and highlight the significance of the former in promoting the latter.

Equal access to education is a reflection of social equity in education, which is an important prerequisite for people to have the opportunity and ability to develop themselves and contribute to society. It is an important element of social equity—the former is aimed to promote the latter. Since the adoption of the reform and opening-up policy, China's huge economic and social achievements have provided solid material foundations and favorable conditions for equal access to education, and social equity and justice. Since the 18th CPC National Congress, our vision of people-centered development has been enacted, initiatives to benefit the people in education have been implemented, all-round progress has been made in education, and access to education has become fairer. Nonetheless, unbalanced and insufficient development still constrains equal access to education in China. There still exist wide education gaps between schools, urban and rural areas, and regions. To promote equal access to education in the new era, we should take the promotion of social equity and justice and the wellbeing of the people as a mirror, through which we can examine the structure, institutions, policies, and regulations on education, and build up institutions that protect equal access to education, including equal access to opportunities. We should improve the structure and institutions for equal access to education and improve the environment for social equity to achieve fairer education.

Equal access to education is an important means of achieving social equity. The CPC Central Committee with Xi Jinping at the core fully realizes the importance of education equity. It proposed at the 19th CPC National Congress to promote education equity for improving people's wellbeing and social development. With economic and social progress, the degree and level of education has become an important factor affecting career choices, incomes, and social achievements. Promoting equal access to education and ensuring people's equal participation in and right to development is of significance to achieving social equity and justice. Xi Jinping's proposals of changing the future of children through knowledge acquisition and of not letting children from poor families fail at the starting line of life are meant to ensure fairness at the starting point of life through education so that everyone may excel.

## 3.2 Facilitating equal access to good education and improving well-rounded development of the people

Building a moderately prosperous society in all respects and adhering to people-centered development of education call for the provision of fair access to good education. Xi Jinping has reiterated that we should see that each and every child has equal access to good education. Education equity and education quality are two things in unity. Equity must be based on quality, and quality must embody equity. Since the 18th CPC National Congress, the country has been committed to promoting equal access to education, making the shift from quantitative expansion to quality improvement, and meeting the growing and diverse needs of different groups. Major progress has been made in education equity. The educational development in central and western regions has accelerated, the conditions of education in rural areas have improved significantly, the enrolment of students from poor rural areas at key colleges and universities has expanded, and the financial aid system has helped more students in need complete their studies, so that they can have better development and a brighter future in their career.

The well-rounded development of our people requires character education; it is the foundation for the progress of a country and a nation, and determines their future. Xi Jinping has noted, during his visit to Beijing Bayi School, that character education is the core of education, which should be people-centered. According to him, we should teach students in accordance with their aptitudes. Study and practice, and knowledge and action, should go hand in hand, and we should encourage students' wish for innovation and skills. Character education, aiming at students' all-round development and the improvement of the education level of the nation, reflects the CPC's education policy and the requirements of equal access to good education. Since the 1990s, China's implementation of character education for all students has ensured the largest number of children's right to education, and improved education quality and the well-rounded development of the people. To develop character education in the new era, we should innovate education methods, improve talent training, create an environment conducive to the growth of innovative talent, and cultivate hundreds of millions of high-caliber talent as needed by the times. Improving the education of the people is a responsibility of the whole society. Families, schools, governments, and society should create favorable conditions for the development of those being educated so that they can grow up to be pillars of society.

### 3.3 Opportunities for all to excel

Everyone in a socialist country expects to enjoy equal right to education, and to pursue excellence through various types of education. Xi Jinping, when addressing the First Session of the 12th National People's Congress held in 2013, said, "All the Chinese who live in our great country in this great age share the opportunity to pursue excellence, realize our dreams, and develop ourselves along with our country."[1] We should help them improve their physique, enrich their knowledge, and raise their employability. We should provide opportunities for children to have a better future through learning, and for the young and the middle-aged to find suitable jobs, so that they can live a decent life. Xi also emphasized the importance of guaranteeing the right to education for relocated children of migrant workers, left-behind children in rural areas, and children with disabilities, so that every child will gain equal

---

1 Xi Jinping: *The Governance of China*, Vol. I, Foreign Languages Press, Beijing, 2018, p. 42.

access to good education and then serve society.

We should create an environment of learning in which everyone can achieve success while displaying their talent. Together with hundreds of millions of fellow Chinese, they will realize their lifelong dreams. Everyone in society is a worker and has to create a colorful life with their own hands. Work is the source of happiness; it makes living possible and life meaningful. There is still much to do and a long way to go before we realize the Chinese Dream and create a better life for all, so every one of us should work toward this goal as hard as possible. We should develop a correct understanding of talent, make room for everyone to grow, improve the quality of talent training, and build the structures and institutions to ensure that everyone excels. We should encourage everyone to acquire new knowledge, pick up new skills, and develop new competencies while integrating their patriotism and their aspiration to make the country strong. We should foster the concept of equality for all, improve the social status and treatment of professional and skilled workers at all levels, promote the reform of technical and vocational education, and train a large number of skilled workers who are physically and mentally strong. We should help them embrace the spirit of craftsmanship and make commitment to serving the country, so that they are able to do their parts in the cause of building socialism with Chinese characteristics in the new era and fulfil their lifetime expectations.

---

### ✺ Quote from Xi Jinping ✺

We should increase the support for technical and vocational education in rural, poor, and ethnic minority areas, and give everyone the chance to pursue excellence in life.

—Speech on accelerating the development of technical and vocational education, June 23, 2014

---

We will excel if we take the right path, marching forward with our motherland and our fellow countrymen. Socialist education is a cause for all and should be cared about by all. We should all be part of the socialist education with Chinese characteristics in the new era, share weal and woe with the people, and maximize our life values. The people are the creators of history and the masters of the country. Young students, as the new generation shouldering the mission of national rejuvenation, must unite with the people, absorb nutrients from their great practices and colorful life, and defend their fundamental interests. With ambitions, one can reach any place however far it is, even over mountains and across seas. All new generations for the socialist cause should take on the responsibilities entrusted by the new era, work hard at their own posts, start with themselves and from small things, and create their own splendid life through hard work, outstanding performance, and remarkable achievements.

# Chapter 7

**Invigorating Education Through Reform and Innovation**

Those who reform, progress; those who innovate, prosper; those who do both, prevail. Reform and opening up is the unique development path enabling the Communist Party of China and the Chinese people to keep up with the times. It is the only path to uphold and develop socialism with Chinese characteristics. It is a game-changing strategy in the making of contemporary China, and a determinant in the realization of the Two Centenary Goals and the great rejuvenation of the Chinese nation. Following the 18th CPC National Congress, General Secretary Xi Jinping mapped out strategic education reform in the wider context of comprehensive deepening of reform. He has pointed out that reform is the mainspring of educational development. Major problems as well as hot topics in education ought to be studied to provide timely solutions, so as to reinvigorate education in the new era. Openness in education ought to be further expanded to facilitate exchange and cooperation with first-class universities in the world. All these serve to enhance the global influence of China's education. Xi Jinping's remarks on furthering education reform and innovation is a call to act collectively in shaping educational development in the new era.

# 1. Reform as the Mainspring of Educational Development

The thrust of comprehensive deepening of reform sets forth the basic policy in upholding and developing socialism with Chinese characteristics in the new era. In an exclusive interview with Rossiya 1 TV Channel in February 2014, President Xi Jinping pointed out that China, with a population of more than 1.3 billion, faces a herculean task in deepening reform. Reform in China has now entered uncharted waters. It is fair to say that the easy part of the reform has been completed to the satisfaction of all. The low-hanging fruits have been harvested. Now we are ready to crack the tough nuts and that demands bold action in prudent move. We should be bold enough to deal with whatever may come and steer through treacherous waters. We should be prudent enough to ensure steady steps on the right track, make continuous progress, and, above all, avoid fatal mistakes. Since the 18th CPC National Congress, Xi Jinping has presided over meetings of the Central Leading Group for Deepening Reform and the Central Commission for Deepening Reform, deliberating and passing a series of important documents concerning education reform and development. This has encouraged in-depth education reform and innovation.

## 1.1 Invigorating education through reform

Reform holds the key to the next phase of development in education. Each major reform, as seen in the four decades of reform and opening up, has been instilling new vigor and vitality into the Party and the state, and powering up the forward thrust of advancement. Education is not only the forerunner but also the beneficiary and facilitator of China's reform and opening up. Efforts in reform and innovation as promoting education equity and improving education quality underpinned China's achievements in education thus far. Deeper education reform and innovation raised China's overall level of education significantly, which now ranks above the world average. Correspondingly, education can better meet the needs of economic and social development and its international influence is rising. This has expedited the process of making China a country rich in human resources.

Reform at the front lines of education has ignited innovation in education for the new era. "Follow not the beaten path to bring benefits to the people; observe not old conventions to get things done."[1] Reform itself is a process of replacing the old with the new, and education reform is no different. Many problems with relatively easy solutions have been resolved. The attention now falls on thorny and overarching challenges, of which reform of the examination and enrolment systems, as well as the separation of education management, school administration, and educational evaluation stands out. Confronted with emerging problems in the new era, the strong leadership of the CPC Central Committee with Xi Jinping at the core has united the front lines of education to remain steadfast in carrying through reform, inspire innovation, further all-round reform, and progress steadily toward meeting the expectations of the people.

Education reform is pushed forward for the establishment of multiple pillars supporting the institution of education. With great foresight and determined to make progress, the Central Committee with Xi Jinping at the core drew up new plans built on past achievements soon after the 18th CPC National Congress. The overall plan for education reform is framed within the Five-Sphere Integrated Plan and the Four-Pronged Comprehensive Strategy. Focusing on strengthening and

---

1 Cited from *Huainanzi* by Liu An (179-122 BC), who was a man of letters and famous thinker in the Western Han dynasty (206 BC-25 AD).

refining top-level system design and removing institutional obstacles that impede the scientific development of education, the CPC Central Committee and the State Council have formulated a series of recommendations and plans, starting a new journey of education reform. These include deeper reform of the examination and enrolment systems, accelerating the development of modern technical and vocational education and education for ethnic minorities, reforming education institutions, standardizing the development of pre-school education, advancing the integration of compulsory education in urban and rural areas, and stepping up the modernization of China's education, among other important issues. With reform in the examination and enrolment systems as a breakthrough point, all fields and areas have seen all-round progress. Advances in reform are thought out and executed in accordance with the rule of law and guaranteed by the law. To this end, revisions to the following laws were enacted: the Education Law of the People's Republic of China, the Higher Education Law of the People's Republic of China, and the Law of the People's Republic of China on Promoting Non-Government Funded Education.

## 1.2 Solving major problems and handling hot issues in education reform

Reform is a response to meet the expectations of the people. During the visit to Beijing Bayi School, Xi Jinping urged Party committees and governments at all levels to continue to prioritize education in their strategic plans, strengthen their sense of responsibility, study and solve major problems, and handle hot issues in a timely manner. Solving China's real problems has always been the purpose of communist revolution, development, and reform. Reform is launched in response to challenges and deepened in the continual course of problem-solving. Only through vigorous reform and development can we meet the people's needs for better education.

Issues and problems represent the call of the times. They must be the starting point of reform and must be resolved in light of the ultimate goal of education reform. In general, education in China conforms to its overall national conditions and largely fulfils the needs of economic and social development. Considerable work, however, remains to be done given the multi-faceted complexity of education reform. Striking problems include head-start and overlearning in pre-school and basic education, sub-par quality of technical and vocational and higher education, and underdeveloped continuing education. Education equity and quality remain the concerns of the general public. Educational evaluation is another thorny issue beset by a host of deep-rooted assessment maladies of relying solely on grades, admission rates, diplomas, academic papers, and professional titles. To top it all, various institutional barriers are standing in the way of educational development, awaiting further institutional reform in governance and school operation. All in all, impetus has to be created to spur real change and more education endeavor, and to raise the capacity of education to serve economic and social development needs. Only through reform and innovation can education be more accorded with the development of the times, more fitting to the talent requirements of socialism with Chinese characteristics, more conforming to laws of educational development and talent cultivation, and more satisfying to people's keen hopes for better education.

In addressing major and urgent issues, we must adopt a people-centered approach to development, focusing our efforts on alleviating pain points and cracking hard nuts. Since the 18th CPC National Congress, Xi Jinping has issued multiple instructions on education by putting himself in the place of the people. The General Secretary has remained concerned with issues such as school selection fever, large class size, reform of the examination and enrolment systems, and reform of the education institutions and mechanisms. Efforts to resolve these items of concern underscore the consolidation and elaboration of the achievements in education reform attained thus far. Not only is this a litmus test of both the healthy progress of education in China and the people's increased sense of gain in education, it is also a duty to our future that the education sector cannot shirk. In tackling these challenges, we have to cut through complexity, trace down to the part that has the most wide-ranging implications in the overall education plan, and take the bull by the horns.

---

⌒⌒ *Quote from Xi Jinping* ⌒⌒

The great spirit of reform and opening up, which is born out of our four decades of endeavor, has significantly enriched our national character and become the most prominent hallmark of the Chinese people in modern days.

—Speech at the Conference Celebrating the 40th Anniversary of Reform and Opening Up, December 18, 2018

---

Education reform is an ongoing process. Reform conforms to the trend of history and wish of the people. To stop or reverse the reform will lead us nowhere. We must constantly improve ourselves, innovate, and overcome any obstacles on the way. Since the resumption of the college entrance examination system in 1977, China has solved a series of problems in education through reform. While old problems have been fixed, new ones keep emerging. Reform is akin to a profound revolution, initiating change in institutional mechanisms, and breaking down the stronghold of vested interests. Education reform must be boosted by the courage to break open a pathway amid difficulties and the perseverance to forge ahead. It should tackle long-standing, deep-rooted problems and be carried through to the end. Reform cannot be accomplished overnight, nor can it be achieved once and for all. Conflicts resulting from reform may only be solved through more reform. Education reform is a never ending process.

## 1.3 Taking a systematic, holistic, and coordinated approach to education reform

He who does not align to the big picture is not able to manage even one sector well. Xi Jinping explained, "Comprehensively deepening reform means coordinating and advancing reform in all fields."[1] Considering education as an important pillar of Chinese socialism, education reform is not confined to problems in education itself but has much to do with various interrelated socio-economic problems. The tasks of education reform in the new era are much more complex and arduous. They must be accomplished through systematic, holistic, and coordinated efforts, which are inherent requirements for education innovation and important methods to promote education reform.

The systematic approach to strengthening top-level design holds the key to extensive education reform and innovation. There must be a clear understanding of the correlation of reform efforts for various facets at various levels to ensure that reform drive at subsystems is in alignment with the conceptual design. We must treat both root causes and symptoms, and facilitate breakthroughs with periodic outcomes. The Communist Party of China proposes complementing top-level design with hands-on experience, and overall progress with breakthroughs in key areas. This is an important principle that we must follow while comprehensively deepening reform. Education reform has entered a critical stage—uncharted waters of an enmeshed nature within a wider context, which makes it more difficult to solve deep-seated conflicts and problems. The solutions to many problems often involve the responsibilities and functions of multiple departments, supporting policies, and shifts in the interests of various entities. Reliance on the usual mode of isolated reform solution or partial breakthrough no longer works. We should approach reform systematically, holistically and with a global perspective, design reform by considering all relevant factors, and advance it with coordinated planning. We must foster a growing sense of reform, boost confidence in education reform, shatter outdated stereotypes, and break down vested interests to carry through deeper reform progressively throughout the facets of education.

---

1 Xi Jinping: *On Persisting in Comprehensively Deepening Reform*, Chinese edition, Central Party Literature Press, Beijing, 2018, p. 88.

Education reform and innovation should conform to the laws of education and talent cultivation. Xi Jinping has pointed out, "We should improve our talent training mechanisms in accordance with the inherent laws of talent cultivation. We should 'accord a tree with the regularities in its environmental conditions to allow the manifestation of its nature,'[1] avoiding seeking quick success and instant results, or 'helping shoots grow by pulling seedlings up.'"[2] Effective reform enables education at all levels and of all types to better conform to the laws of education and talent cultivation, building a dynamic, efficient, and more open institutional mechanism conducive to high-quality education.

## 2. Deepening Comprehensive Reform in Education

Deepening comprehensive reform in education in the new era is a new requirement set by the Communist Party of China and the state, and it is based on the Five-Sphere Integrated Plan and the Four-Pronged Comprehensive Strategy. During his visit to Beijing Bayi School, Xi Jinping pointed out that we should deepen the reform of the systems of school running, administration, funding, examination, enrolment, employment, human resources, salary, and teaching administration, as well as the reform of talent training modes, teaching content, and pedagogical methods. At the National Education Conference, he further emphasized the need to change the current problematic guiding principles of education evaluation and find a fundamental solution for the assessment. He noted that we should drive deeper reform

---

1 Cited from "The Story of the Tree Planter Guo Tuotuo" by Liu Zongyuan (773-819), a poet, prose writer, and thinker of the Tang dynasty (618-907).
2 Xi Jinping: *Speech at the 17th Meeting of the Members of the Chinese Academy of Sciences and the 12th Meeting of the Members of the Chinese Academy of Engineering*, Chinese edition, People's Publishing House, Beijing, 2014, p. 18.

in school operating mechanisms and education management to fully release the vigor of education. Key areas of development include: cultivating innovative, interdisciplinary, and professional personnel with practical skills; expanding the capacity of education in serving economic and social growth; prioritizing the model to "teach well," "learn well," and "manage well," to remodel the underlying education institution and raise standards. These are fresh signposting ideas and conclusions.

## 2.1 Promoting innovation in talent training modes

Talent is the brain that makes a country thriving, governance stable, and business prosperous. Talent is the source of innovation, and nurturing, attracting, and retaining talent is entrenched in innovation. During the ninth group study session of the Political Bureau of the 18th CPC Central Committee in 2013, Xi Jinping emphasized the need to deepen education reform, promote character education, innovate education methods, improve the quality of talent training, and strive to form an education environment conducive to the growth of innovative talent. That is to say, the reform and innovation should focus on creating institutions conducive to the growth of talent.

*Establishing the right concept on talent training.* Talent training in the new era should embrace the concept of comprehensive development. We should establish an education system that fosters all-round moral, intellectual, physical, and aesthetic development with a love for labor. It is necessary to establish the attitude of "making everyone the talent he is capable of," and to help students to increase intellectual growth. It is also necessary to establish the concept of valuing talent diversity, with which talented individuals are taught to use approaches tailored to their aptitudes. The concept of lifelong learning should be established to lay the foundation for sustainable development. We should establish the idea of systematic training, promoting systematic curricular links from primary schools through universities, effective integration of teaching, research, and practice, and close coordination among schools, families, the government, and society. Various joint training methods, such as partnership between schools, between schools and enterprises, between schools and scientific research institutions, and between Chinese and foreign entities, should be strengthened to form a talent training system that is open and has flexible mechanisms, interconnected channels, and diverse choices.

*Innovating teaching methods and improving the quality of talent training.* We should teach students according to their aptitudes. Just as no two leaves are identical in the world, within a classroom is a diverse range of personalities, hobbies, temperaments, interests, specialties, family circumstances, and learning status. Teachers must carefully guide and cultivate students to meet their different needs while treating them all equitably. Learning and thinking should go hand in hand. Whether in school or in society, we should promote the close connection between learning, observing, practicing, and thinking. In addition, we should maintain a keen sense for new things. We should learn to approach problems from perspectives, viewpoints, and methods relevant to the context, and we should cultivate students' problem-solving awareness and ability. Knowledge must be applied in practice. Knowledge obtained by students must not remain abstract notions or be kept in mind only, but should be put into practice. Knowledge and practice should be united, with knowledge guiding practice and practice generating new knowledge. Whereas theory and practice should complement each other, teaching should relate to productive labor and social activities.

## 2.2 Deepening reform in school operation and education management

China has the largest education system in the world, but it is particularly complex, as there is uneven development between urban and rural areas and among different regions, as well as differences in the educational needs of the people. Xi Jinping has pointed out, "In order to run and develop this large and complex sector well, we must further our reform in school operating mechanism and education management, modernize our capacity, and raise the level of governance in education by addressing such problems as inadequacy in self-restraint and self-development of schools; excessive, deficient, improper or under-performing governance of schools by governments; and lack of social participation."[1] At present, education reform is at a critical stage, and mechanisms for education management have become the "hard nuts" of reform. For example, the relationships between the government, schools, and society have yet to be clarified; the enthusiasm of schools and society to participate in education needs further stimulus; and the educational rights and responsibilities of governments at different levels need to be further defined. In addition, education management modes need to be more scientific. Targeting these problems, it is necessary to deepen the reform of the school running system and management system by aligning them to the goal of improving and developing the socialist education system with Chinese characteristics and modernizing education governance system and capacity.

An important part of this reform is the streamlining of administration and delegation of authority, while strengthening supervision and raising service standards in an effort to redefine the interactions between the government, schools, and society. We will further streamline administration and distribute authority downward by accelerating the transformation of government functions, respecting the laws of education, and providing quality services for education. To this end, schools shall be given, as far as practicable, the right to allocate resources, use funds, and manage evaluation and assessment. Their roles as principal actors should be respected. It is necessary to refine the internal administrative structures of schools and to form internal management systems, as well as supervision and restriction mechanisms of self-restraint and self-regulation. We will urge community-level organizations and schools to refine their systems of school operation, strengthen their mechanisms of strict school governance, and constantly improve their systems for education management and services. While respecting the laws of

---

1  Xi Jinping: *On Persisting in Comprehensively Deepening Reform*, Chinese edition, Central Party Literature Press, Beijing, 2018, p. 474.

educational development, we should encourage the non-governmental sector to run education programs within the framework of law, give full play to the role of schools at all levels and of all types as the principal actors in school administration, significantly reduce various types of inspection, assessment, and evaluation, and strengthen normative guidance on the direction, standards, and quality of school operation. This will create a favorable environment for school running.

We should dive deep into the reform of school operation to reinvigorate educational institutions. The goal is to mobilize society-wide participation and revitalize the education sector to meet the multi-layered and diverse educational needs of the people. Educational institutions are like cells making up the education system and the reform of school operation is oriented toward sustainable and healthy development of schools, keeping the "cells" lively. Only by serving the society and constantly improving the ability and level of service can schools achieve sound and sustainable development.

Education reform and education governance in accordance with the law are like the two wheels of a cart or the two wings of a bird. In the entire process of reform, we must always accept the guidance of law and apply law-based thinking and approaches. Reform is of overall consequence. We must remove the institutional obstacles that hinder the scientific development of education, and coordinate reforms with economic, political, cultural, and social development, and ecological progress. We must ensure that relevant laws are made and observed in education governance and in the establishment and operation of schools. Education reform is at a crossroads, entering uncharted waters, and the role of legislation is crucial to the smooth progress of reform, and more importantly, to the consolidation and sustainability of reformative achievements. To realize law-based education governance, we should develop a complete, well-designed and structured, and effective legal system of education, and form an implementation and supervision system in which government administration, school operation, teaching activities, and social evaluation, support, and oversight all take place under the rule of law.

## 2.3 Using proper evaluation to steer education

> **⟡ Quote from Xi Jinping ⟡**
>
> Be resolute to overcome the deep-rooted problems of relying solely on grades, admission rates, diplomas, academic papers, and professional titles, and remove their excessive influence on the evaluation of education.
>
> —Speech at the National Education Conference, September 10, 2018

Evaluation criteria guide the operation of schools. As Xi Jinping pointed out, "The current yardstick for education is scores and admission rates for primary and secondary schools, and research papers for colleges and universities. We have yet to accord moral education and character education their rightful places in school evaluation, and that is where we are in need of a scientific evaluation system. This perennial and difficult problem must be solved."[1] We should revamp our evaluation systems for schools, teachers, students, and education, and we should change the simplistic practice of evaluating teachers via test rankings, of evaluating students via exam scores, and of evaluating schools via admission rates. We must resolutely stop the practice of rewarding or penalizing schools according to admission rates, and we should end the practice of linking admission rates with the allocation of various resources. Extracurricular training institutions should be managed according to the law so that such training can perform its fundamental task of educating people.

We must further the reform of examination and enrolment systems to redress the deep-seated problems in educational evaluation. Examination and enrolment systems are basic national education systems. They affect the future of hundreds of millions of young students, and they

---

1 Xi Jinping: *On Persisting in Comprehensively Deepening Reform*, Chinese edition, Central Party Literature Press, Beijing, 2018, pp. 472-473.

also affect the forming of China's talent pool and its development plan. Therefore, this is a key area and a crucial link in education reform that has a ripple effect on national issues. On the whole, existing examination and enrolment systems conform with China's national conditions, but they also have some shortcomings, such as overburdening students, regional, urban, and rural gaps in school access, and competition for vacancy in good public schools during compulsory education. Further reform efforts should promote fairness in education and improve talent selection, as this will meet the requirements for training new generations of socialist builders with all-round moral, intellectual, physical, and aesthetic development and with a love for labor.

Deepening reform of examination and enrolment systems should be realized through the formation of an examination and enrolment model characterized by subject-specific examination, comprehensive evaluation, and diversified admission criteria. We must improve the institution mechanisms to ensure fair and effective competition and supervision, and devise a lifelong learning system that connects all types and levels of education and recognizes a wide range of learning outcomes. Substantiated by thorough analysis and top-level design perspective, pilot implementation of revised examination and enrolment systems can be set up and scale up in stages methodically. We must conduct a complete survey on the pilot programs and draw specific lessons for improvement. Before rolling out in full, we must constantly adjust and fine-tune the proposed revision and tackle new challenges along the way.

## 3. Further Opening Up Education to Enhance Its Global Influence

Reform inevitably calls for opening up, which inevitably calls for reform. Pushing forward reform and development through opening up has been successful in China, and a major component of this endeavor is educational opening up. Since the 18th CPC National Congress, the action plan of opening up the education sector has been aligned with the overall work plan of the Party and the state, coordinating relevant domestic-foreign segments and tapping both domestic and international resources to keep raising the quality and standard of opening up education to the outside world. We now have an open education system that is holistic, multi-level, and extensive, showcasing a stronger China with greater global influence.

## 3.1 Drawing on advanced international experience in running schools and conducting academic research

Oceans and rivers owe their water to multiple inlets. In a similar vein, a nation or country should learn from others. China has always aspired to be a learning country. At the National Education Conference, Xi Jinping emphasized that we should open our education sector wider to the outside world, and carry out high-level collaboration in offering education programs with top-notch institutions. Adopting an open and inclusive mindset and a broad perspective, China in the new era is pushing for internal and external development by constantly learning from other countries and peoples to draw on the achievements of their civilizations. In the opening up of China's education in the new era, we must learn from advanced ideas and experience of other countries so as to promote our education reform and development, and enhance the international status, influence, and competitiveness of China's education.

We are committed to cooperation among strong partners to introduce high-quality educational resources and enhance China's educational strength and capacity for innovation. Xi Jinping has pointed out, "We should focus on the world's cutting-edge science and technology as well as domestic disciplines that are weak, absent, or in short supply. We should carry out high-level cooperation in running schools with world-class resources and bring in high-quality ones that meet our needs."[1] We should attract well-known overseas schools, as well as educational and research institutions and enterprises, to set up joint education, teaching, training, and research institutions or projects. We should continue to extend the process of opening up in education while relaxing restrictions on foreign equity ownership in the education sector. We should encourage schools at all levels and of all types to conduct various forms of international exchange and cooperation, and we will ensure the success of the partnership programs. We should attach great importance to introducing world-class universities and disciplines, draw on the advanced management experience of world-class universities, improve internal governance structures, and accelerate the construction of a modern university system with Chinese characteristics.

Regarding talent training, universities should participate in major international science programs and projects, build high-level joint international laboratories and joint international research centers, bring in high-level innovative talent from around the world, and promote international collaborative innovation in science and technology among universities. We must also select and send outstanding young teachers and academic leaders from institutions of higher education to prestigious institutions abroad for exchange programs, and we must invite more teachers from world-renowned universities to China while accelerating the establishment of high-caliber teacher teams of our own. We should cultivate talented people with a global vision who are familiar with policies of the Party and the state, proficient in foreign languages, adept in international rules, and skillful in negotiation and communication with foreign parties. We should train professional, technical, and managerial personnel proficient in foreign languages ready to serve the Belt and Road Initiative. We should nurture and encourage outstanding individuals to apply for positions with international organizations.

---

1 Xi Jinping: *On Persisting in Comprehensively Deepening Reform*, Chinese edition, Central Party Literature Press, Beijing, 2018, p. 475.

## 3.2 Coordinating efforts to serve inbound and outbound study programs

─ ◎ *Quote from Xi Jinping* ◎ ─

If you return to China, there is ample room for you to exercise your abilities. If you remain abroad, you will also have the opportunity to serve your home country.

—Speech at the celebration of the 100th anniversary of the Western Returned Scholars Association, October 21, 2013

In his instructions to the National Conference on Studying Abroad in 2014, Xi Jinping emphasized that in light of current circumstances, the practice of studying overseas should adapt to the general trend of national development and the overall work of the Party and the state. In addition, inbound and outbound study programs should be coordinated and well planned, as both domestic and international resources should be comprehensively utilized to train more outstanding talent. Finally, efforts should be made to create new opportunities for studying abroad, making new and greater contributions to realizing the Two Centenary Goals and the Chinese Dream of national rejuvenation. Since the 18th CPC National Congress, China has maintained its position as the world's largest source of students studying abroad, and it has seen a significant increase in the number of returnees as well as a steady improvement in the quality of educational cooperation and exchanges with other countries.

At the celebration marking the 100th anniversary of the Western Returned Scholars Association, and in light of the strategy of invigorating China through science, education, and talent, Xi Jinping proposed a policy that supports overseas studies, encourages returns, guarantees the freedom of leaving, and promises a role to play, further clarifying the guiding principles for studying abroad. We must provide better services, strengthen education and guidance, and create a working mechanism for the selection, dispatching, management, returning, and employment of government-sponsored overseas students. Similarly, we must adopt new approaches in talent recruitment, attract prospective talent from overseas, and create a favorable environment for Chinese studying and working abroad to return home and serve the country, and an environment that will reward the cream of the crop.

The policy pinpoints new changes, problems, and trends regarding studying abroad in the new era, and highlights the importance of social benefits of sending students to study abroad for enhancing social development, economic growth, national security, and cultural confidence. Xi Jinping hopes that overseas students will remain patriotic, study hard, strive for innovation and creativity, and promote foreign exchanges. Overseas Chinese students should combine their patriotism with devotion, and put it into action to serve the country. They may weld their personal dreams with the Chinese Dream, and be motivated to leave their names in the annals of the great rejuvenation of the Chinese nation.

We will build a strong brand of "Study in China." Xi Jinping points out, "As part of our efforts to train global elites for the future, we should develop internationally competitive education to attract outstanding students from around the world, thus making China a major world education center and a sought-after destination for international students."[1] Therefore, we need to improve service mechanisms and supervision systems for studying in China, and encourage qualified schools and research institutions to participate in the education of international students in accordance with the law. After the 18th CPC National Congress, in service of our international relations and opening up of education to the outside world, a specialized service system for studying in China was established. The system has optimized the source countries of students and academic disciplines and strengthened branded majors and courses. The number of students studying in China has continued to rise, and their education quality has steadily improved.

---

1 Xi Jinping: *On Persisting in Comprehensively Deepening Reform*, Chinese edition, Central Party Literature Press, Beijing, 2018, pp. 475-476.

Studying in China is increasingly appealing as the country grows in its economy and overall national strength. China has become Asia's largest choice destination for international students.

### 3.3 Promoting international cooperation and people-to-people exchange in education

"Friendship, which derives from close contact between peoples, holds the key to sound state-to-state relations."[1] Cultural exchange is a bridge of friendship between peoples, a driving force for social progress, and a bond for regional and world peace. To succeed in modernizing education, we must open up to the outside world and strengthen inclusiveness, mutual learning, and communication with other countries. In his congratulatory letter to the launch ceremony of the Schwarzman Scholars Program at Tsinghua University in 2013, Xi Jinping pointed out that today's world is a community with a shared future. To overcome the various challenges facing human development, people of all countries must work together and help each other. Education should follow this trend, and through closer interaction and exchange, it should promote a better understanding of all kinds of human knowledge and cultures, as well as a better understanding of the current efforts and future aspirations of all nations. Then students from all over the world can increase their mutual understanding, develop a global perspective, inspire creativity in each other, and establish the ambition of contributing wisdom and strength to the peace and development of humanity. Educational opening up should promote cultural and educational exchanges with other countries. It should promote mutual understanding between peoples and mutual learning between civilizations, and make educational cooperation a pioneer of people-to-people and cultural exchanges between China and other countries. Since the 18th CPC

---

1 Cited from *Hanfeizi*. Hanfeizi (*c.* 280-233 BC), the author, was a thinker and philosopher in the late Warring States Period (475-221 BC).

National Congress, people-to-people and cultural exchanges between China and other countries have developed in leaps and bounds. Education has played a positive role in promoting mutual understanding and friendship among peoples of all countries, and in promoting the development of international relations. It is an important way to consolidate public support for relations between China and other countries, and to improve the level of China's opening up to the outside world.

We must tell China's story well and make its voice heard. Educational opening up undertakes the duty and task of enhancing trust, dispelling doubts, connecting China with the rest of the world, and spreading Chinese ideas. We must encourage overseas Chinese students to communicate China's achievements to their host countries, let foreign teachers and students play an active role in bridging gaps, and actively promote cultural exchanges between China and other countries. Confucius Institutes are important platforms for the world to learn more about China, and important links between the Chinese people and other peoples around the world. Xi Jinping pointed out at the opening ceremony of the annual meeting of Confucius Institutes and Confucius Classrooms across the UK in 2015 that, as a window and a bridge for language and cultural exchanges between China and foreign countries, Confucius Institutes and Confucius Classrooms have played a positive role in helping people around the world learn the Chinese language and learn more about Chinese culture. They have also made an important contribution to promoting people-to-people and cultural exchanges between China and other countries, as well as to promoting the development of diverse world civilizations. To promote educational and cultural exchanges between China and foreign countries, we should attach great importance to the development of Confucius Institutes, build more overseas international schools with Chinese characteristics, and encourage qualified technical and vocational colleges to establish Luban Workshops[1] overseas.

---

1 A Luban Workshop is a polytechnic workshop named after Luban, a skilled carpenter in ancient China.

We must promote educational cooperation via the Belt and Road Initiative. The Belt and Road Initiative builds on the heritage of the ancient Silk Road. People-to-people and cultural exchanges and cooperation are an important element of the Belt and Road whose true success hinges upon mutual appreciation, understanding, and respect among the peoples along the route. This initiative by China has delivered benefits to the rest of the world. With the extension of the Belt and Road, China's education will open up further to the world, and invite deeper understanding of China's story. At the eighth meeting of the CPC Central Leading Group for Financial and Economic Affairs in 2014, Xi Jinping pointed out that the Belt and Road Initiative should promote economic cooperation and people-to-people and cultural exchanges in education, tourism, academia, and art in particular between China and other Belt and Road countries. To promote Belt and Road educational cooperation, we should accelerate the training of top international talent, improve the policies to attract overseas students returning to China to start businesses or seek jobs, improve the standard of education programs jointly set up by Chinese and foreign entities, and improve the entry and exit mechanisms for such joint cooperation. We should strengthen educational cooperation with countries along the Belt and Road, and build a comprehensive Belt and Road platform for educational resources and information services. In addition, we should establish an international platform for scientific and educational cooperation and exchange, and implement an action plan for the Belt and Road Initiative facilitated by the scientific and technological innovation of institutions of higher education. We should increase people-to-people and cultural exchanges with other countries along the Belt and Road, support non-governmental exchanges between China and other countries, and strengthen exchanges in sports, art, and other fields. Finally, more efforts should be made to promote the teaching of Chinese as a foreign language.

> ### ～Quote from Xi Jinping～
>
> Civilization becomes colorful through exchanges, and civilization is enriched through mutual learning.
>
> —Speech at the UNESCO headquarters in Paris, March 27, 2014

We should participate in global governance of education. In the new era, China is moving closer to the center stage of the world and making a greater contribution to the progress of humanity. The country believes in upholding the global governance principles of extensive consultation, joint contribution, and shared benefits. As a responsible country, it will take an active part in reforming and developing the global governance system by contributing its wisdom and strength. We will strengthen the international exchange and cooperation framework in education by building pragmatic partnerships with major countries, neighboring countries, developing countries, as well as international organizations. This strategy would enhance development in key areas of education and deliver win–win results through opening up. We endeavor to undertake international responsibilities, provide international assistance in education, and help developing countries to train specialized personnel. We will take an active part in the multilateral educational initiatives of UNESCO and other UN agencies as well as other international organizations, and put forward new ideas, initiatives, and plans for the development of global education. Likewise, we will participate in the formulation of international educational rules and standards. In the new era, China's education will be more open to the world. Similarly, it will more actively participate in the governance of global education, and share Chinese wisdom in overcoming obstacles in the development of world education.

# Chapter 8

## The Importance of Talent and Education for National Rejuvenation

General Secretary Xi Jinping delineated the important aim of education at the National Education Conference: education is a critical means of achieving the goal of rejuvenating the Chinese nation. As such, the capacity of education to serve economic and social progress should be strengthened in the overall implementation of the Five-Sphere Integrated Plan and the Four-Pronged Comprehensive Strategy. Xi's exposition on the aim of education has refreshed our understanding and offered an elevated view of the historic mission attached to education. It provides guidance for the country to modernize its education, and transform itself into an educational powerhouse in the new era.

## 1. Building an Educational Powerhouse: the Foundation for National Rejuvenation

On November 29, 2012, the National Museum of China welcomed a special group of visitors—Xi Jinping and his colleagues on the Standing Committee of the Political Bureau of the CPC Central Committee—just 15 days after Xi took office as General Secretary. They were guided through the exhibition entitled *The Road of Rejuvenation*. Pictures, charts, physical objects, and videos brought back the years of sweeping changes since the dawn of modern China in the 1840s. During this visit, Xi Jinping remarked that the exhibition, which reviewed China's past, showed its present, and declared its future, was informative and inspiring. Quoting a few lines, he said that we had "stormed strong passes[1] and come a long way"; we were "turning seas into mulberry fields";[2] and we would "advance through winds and waves."[3] He pointed out that the full rejuvenation of the Chinese nation has been China's greatest dream since the advent of modern times. This dream has been cherished by several generations of Chinese people. It represents the overall interests of the Chinese nation and the common aspiration of the Chinese people.

---

1 Cited from Mao Zedong's poem "Loushan Pass," meaning not being afraid of the difficulties ahead.
2 Cited from Mao Zedong's poem "The People's Liberation Army Occupied Nanjing," meaning that constant change and progress are the inevitable law of social development.
3 Cited from "Three Poems of Traveling's Hard (I)" written by Li Bai (701-762) of the Tang dynasty (618-907), meaning that people should be confident enough to ride winds and break waves.

Education plays a vital role in the rejuvenation of the Chinese nation. Focusing on international competition and the overall trend of China's development, Xi Jinping has stated that to make China a country strong in education is fundamental for national rejuvenation. This observation has set the goal for education in the new era, and represents a theoretical innovation that recognizes the position and mission of education.

## 1.1 Education: the key to national rejuvenation

The contest for overall national strength in the world today is a competition for talent. Talented people are the lifeblood of nations. Xi Jinping has pointed out that talent is an important indicator of a country's overall national strength, and the strategic resource for realizing national rejuvenation and gaining the initiative in international competition. To possess a large pool of talented people and make the best use of their talents are prerequisites for a large and strong country, and an important support for a country's long-term prosperity. In today's world, the functions of talented people as the primary resource of economic and social development have become ever more obvious. Competition for talent has become the core in the competition of overall national strength. Whoever can train and attract more talent will gain advantage in this competition. Experience in various countries has shown that the more advanced the modernization drive, the more urgent the need for talent. The more talented people there are, and the more effective roles they play, the faster modernization will proceed.

---

#### ❧ *Quote from Xi Jinping* ❧

Both hard and soft powers ultimately depend on talent.

—Speech at the 19th Meeting of the Members of the Chinese Academy of Sciences and the 14th Meeting of the Members of the Chinese Academy of Engineering, May 28, 2018

---

In the current era, the thirst for scientific knowledge and outstanding talent has grown more intense. A comprehensive review of international and domestic trends shows that China is still in an important period of strategic opportunity in which much can be achieved. When the right time comes, don't miss it; when an opportunity knocks, seize it.[1] Now, we are closer to the goal of national rejuvenation than at any other time in history, and we are more confident about and capable of realizing this goal than at any other time. Xi Jinping has emphasized, "The realization of the Two Centenary Goals and the Chinese Dream of national rejuvenation ultimately depends on talent and education."[2] Without a large contingent of talent, it would be difficult to realize the goal of building a moderately prosperous society in all respects and the Chinese Dream of national rejuvenation. At present, reform in China has entered a critical period. We should tackle tough problems and brave great waves. Thus, China must urgently train a large number of innovative, talented personnel and accelerate the building of teams of talent.

At present, there are still many weaknesses in the Chinese education system, and there is still a huge gap between the supply of and demand for talent. Since the 18th CPC National Congress in 2012, the overall development of China's education has been rapid. Likewise, the overall capacity to supply talented people has been enhanced. The international competitiveness of Chinese talent has improved. This has provided solid support for the implementation of major national strategies such as China's innovation-driven development strategy. Additionally, it has promoted scientific and technological innovation as well as cultural prosperity, and made significant contributions to economic development, social progress, and the improvement of people's lives. It should also be noted, however, that socialism with Chinese characteristics has

---

1 Cited from "A Hypothetical Persuasive Letter from Hou to Xiang Yu" by Su Shi (1037-1101) of the Northern Song dynasty (960-1127).

2 Xi Jinping: *Being a Good Teacher to the Satisfaction of the Communist Party of China and the People—Speech at the Meeting with Teachers and Students of Beijing Normal University*, Chinese edition, People's Publishing House, Beijing, 2014, p. 3.

entered a new era and has put forward new and higher requirements for education. Education at present is continuing to expand in scale, but there is still a gap between the demand for talent and China's educational capacity. In particular, the supply of innovative talent needed for social and economic development in the new era is insufficient, and there is still a long way to go to improve the overall competence of the Chinese nation.

To build a great modern socialist country, we must prioritize and modernize our education. Since the reform and opening up in the late 1970s—and especially since the 18th CPC National Congress—China has put forward a series of strategic objectives and tasks for strengthening itself in science, technology, manufacturing, and culture. But no matter what kind of powerhouse we want to build, strong human resources are needed to play the supporting role. Economic progress, political advancement, cultural growth, social evolution, and ecological conservation are all inseparable from human resources development and talent training. Likewise, the implementation of strategies for rural revitalization, coordinated regional development, sustainable development, and the military-civilian integration is also inseparable from the strong support of education. Building an educational powerhouse is the foundation for a great modern socialist country, which is not only strong in a certain field, but in all areas. To build a great modern socialist country, we must be strong politically, economically, militarily, and culturally, and make our education endeavor bigger, stronger, and more successful.

## 1.2 Modernizing education and building a strong education sector

In his report to the 19th CPC National Congress, General Secretary Xi presented the overall strategy of prioritizing education, the way to accelerate education modernization, and the requirements for making China strong in education. "Prioritizing education," "modernizing education," and "building an educational powerhouse"—these initiatives demonstrate the continuity of our education policies while incorporating new requirements in the present circumstances. They are major strategic plans to reform and develop education in the new era.

The 19th CPC National Congress presented a strategic arrangement for socialist modernization. In terms of the timeframe, it has advanced the original schedule for China's socialist modernization by fifteen years. In terms of goals, this plan will transform China from a moderately developed, modern socialist country by the middle of this century into a great modern socialist country that is prosperous, strong, democratic, culturally advanced, harmonious, and beautiful. This suggests not only an increase in quantity, but also a qualitative leap. In terms of requirements, the plan throws further light on the requirements of the Four Consciousnesses, the Four-Sphere Confidence, the Four Greats, the Five-Sphere Integrated Plan, and the Four-Pronged Comprehensive Strategy, and of modernizing China's system and capacity for governance. The strategic plan for building a great modern socialist country made at the 19th CPC National Congress provides the blueprint for modernizing China's education and transforming the country into an educational powerhouse.

From the strategic height of adhering to and developing socialism with Chinese characteristics in the new era, the 19th CPC National Congress laid out the key tasks of prioritizing education, accelerating modernization of education, and making China an educational powerhouse. The report to the 19th CPC National Congress pointed out that it is necessary to fully implement the CPC's education policy, carry out the fundamental task of training people, develop character education, promote fairness in education, and train well-rounded new generations of socialist builders. This clarified the overall direction for education in the new era. The report stated that it is necessary to integrate the development of education in urban and rural areas, attach importance to compulsory education in rural areas, and provide good pre-school education, special education, and online education. It also stated that it is necessary to popularize high school education while striving to ensure that every child has access to a fair and quality education. We must improve technical and vocational education and training systems, and achieve deeper integration of industry and education, as well as closer cooperation between schools and enterprises. We must accelerate the development of first-class universities and disciplines, and achieve quality-based growth of higher education. These requirements are clearly oriented, pointing out the direction of efforts in pre-school, special, online, high school, technical and vocational, and higher education. The report proposed strategic measures to accelerate the building of an innovative country, a nation governed by the rule of law, and a beautiful China, thus setting new and higher requirements for education to serve and contribute to the socialist modernization drive.

The National Education Conference held by the CPC Central Committee in September 2018 was the first of its kind in the context of socialism with Chinese characteristics entering a new era, so it is of landmark significance in the history of China's education. At this conference, Xi Jinping shared his views on major issues concerning China's education modernization. He pointed out that we should seize opportunities and draw up plans well in advance. He also said that we must make overall arrangements and strategic plans to modernize and strengthen education from historical, international, and strategic perspectives. This conference marked a new stage in China's education modernization and a new journey to make the country an educational powerhouse.

Toward the end of 2018, the CPC Central Committee and the State Council issued *China's Education Modernization 2035* and restated the overall goal of education modernization. To that end, the goals of the 13th Five-Year Plan will be completed in 2020. By then, China's overall strength and international influence of education will be significantly enhanced. The average number of years of schooling for the working-age population will be significantly increased, and important progress will be made in modernizing education, thus facilitating the building of a moderately prosperous society in all respects. On this base, after another 15 years of hard work, China will by 2035 have realized the overall modernization of education and enjoyed a strong education sector. China will strive to become a major learning society, rich in human resources and talent, thereby laying a solid foundation for building a great modern socialist country that is prosperous, strong, democratic, culturally advanced, harmonious, and beautiful by the middle of this century. *China's Education Modernization 2035* puts forward the basic principles, overall objectives, strategic tasks, implementation approaches, and enabling measures for education modernization. It provides the direction and guidelines for the new journey of education modernization in the new era.

## 2. Increasing Educators' Sense of Mission for National Rejuvenation

Each era has its own challenges, and each generation has its own mission. Although we have come a long way, we still have an arduous journey ahead. Facing new situations, tasks, and requirements in the new era, we must adhere to the principle of educating people for the CPC and the nation. We must increase the educators' sense of mission for national rejuvenation and make new achievements worthy of the new era through higher standards, stronger skills, finer work styles, and better mental states.

### 2.1 Driving education to meet the needs of the Party and the nation

Xi Jinping pointed out at the National Education Conference of 2018 that it is necessary to continuously drive education to meet the needs of the Party and the nation, as well as meet the expectations of the people and match China's overall national strength and international status. This provides the direction for the development of education in the new era.

Education makes important contributions to the cause of the Party and the country. The education sector must be aligned with the overall requirements for developing the cause of the Party and the country, be aware of the central tasks, bear in mind the big picture, and play a leading, foundational, and comprehensive role. Socialism with Chinese characteristics has entered a new era. This is a new historic juncture in China's development. Built on past successes, the new era will further advance our cause and strive for greater success of socialism with Chinese characteristics under new historical circumstances. It will be an era of securing a decisive victory in building a moderately prosperous society in all respects, and of moving on to all-out efforts to build a great modern socialist country. It will be an era for the Chinese people of all ethnic groups to work together and work hard to create a better life for themselves and ultimately achieve common prosperity for everyone. It will be an era for all of us, the sons and daughters of the Chinese nation, to strive with one heart to realize the Chinese Dream of national rejuvenation. It is an era that sees China moving closer to the center stage of the world and making a greater contribution to humanity. The new era has put forward many new requirements for developing the cause of the Party and the country. Likewise, the development of education must conform to the trend, the characteristics, and the needs of the times.

In the new era, education has reached a new historic juncture. Educational development should meet the needs of China's socialist cause. It should serve the goal of building a moderately prosperous society in all respects, as well as the rejuvenation of the Chinese nation. Education in China should actively adapt to and lead the "new normal" economic development while cultivating talent and fostering a force for innovation in the country's modernization drive. To develop education in line with the needs of the Party and the nation throughout this new historical stage, it is necessary to drive deeper education reform and innovation, and create an education mechanism adapted to economic and social growth. To enable education to meet people's expectations, we must remain people-centered and try to satisfy people's growing needs for a better life. To develop education in line with China's overall national strength and international status, we must accelerate education modernization, make the country an educational powerhouse, and contribute Chinese wisdom to the peaceful development of the world.

To ensure progress toward high-quality education in the new era, it is necessary to integrate education with the goals and needs of national development, which must be planned, deployed, and examined as a whole. As reform goes deeper, new situations and problems will arise, leading to greater risks and challenges. To successfully uphold and develop socialism with Chinese characteristics in the new era, it is necessary to understand the new requirements and constantly strengthen all undertakings of the Party and the state. In the new era, the principal challenge facing Chinese society has evolved, and this is reflected in the change of strategic priorities of the Party and the state. To solve the problem of unbalanced and inadequate development, we need to plan from an overall perspective, think in big-picture terms, and take a holistic view. The future of education should be planned, organized, and coordinated alongside the future of the Party and the state.

## 2.2 Education for bringing benefits to the people

Xi Jinping emphasized at the National Education Conference that education in the new era should be devoted to social cohesion, refining people's character, developing human resources, nurturing talent, and improving lives. This new goal for education is based on the importance of education to the rejuvenation of the Chinese nation. It is a new requirement and positioning for education in the new era. Educational development should consciously take on the important mission of the new era and contribute to the great cause of national rejuvenation.

We must boost social cohesion. Achieving national rejuvenation is the common cause of the CPC, the Chinese nation, and its society. The success of the cause is no simple matter. To realize this great dream, we must make a concerted effort to carry forward China's spirit, spread China's values, and consolidate China's strength. The will and wish of the people mean strength and should lie at the core of all political considerations. To carry out the great struggle for national development, the great project of strengthening our Party, the great cause of Chinese socialism, and to realize the great dream of national rejuvenation in the new era, it is especially necessary for education to play its role in bolstering confidence, rallying people, warming their hearts, and forging solidarity. Education at all levels and of all types should guide the general public toward Xi Jinping Thought on Socialism with Chinese Characteristics for a New Era. It should persevere in uniting us as one and in demonstrating solidarity in times of adversity. We should think and work in concert to forge ahead toward the goal of making China a great modern socialist country in all respects and realizing national rejuvenation.

We need to refine our character. Education in the new era should train new generations who can take on the responsibility for the great task of national rejuvenation. Those involved should be equipped with noble virtues, sound personalities, healthy bodies and minds, and well-rounded development. General Secretary Xi has emphasized that through education, the Chinese nation should be guided from generation to generation to pursue fine and noble morals, and the Chinese people should be guided to develop and uphold the correct views on history, nations, countries, and cultures. We should increase our confidence as Chinese. We should cultivate noble character and a healthy taste for life, and promote aesthetic and cultural literacy for better personalities and well-rounded development.

We must develop human resources. People are the most valuable resource and the source of all innovations. Xi Jinping has pointed out that China has a wealth of human and intellectual resources. The collective wisdom of more than 1.3 billion Chinese people is its most precious asset. We must pay more attention to strengthening education, improving the quality of China's human resources, and investing more in human capital to enhance the quality of education. Education at all levels and of all types must undertake the mission of developing human resources. It is necessary to extend education reform, promote character education, innovate educational methods, improve education quality, and provide support for building human resources who can turn China into a great modern socialist country.

We must foster talent. Xi Jinping has made important observations on the training of specialized personnel in various fields. In science and technology, he has proposed training "a contingent of internationally qualified talent in strategic fields," "science and technology leaders," "young talent in science and technology," and "high-level innovative teams." In philosophy and social sciences, he has proposed building a complete system that is conducive to producing talented individuals in all the fields, at all levels, and of different age groups. In cyber science and technology, he has emphasized the need to be open-minded and welcome talent of all kinds and accelerate the training of leading experts. In the military field, he has stressed the need to develop a new system for training military personnel by deepening the reform of military academies. And regarding the legal sector, he has noted the importance of moral education in legal training to bring up large numbers of high-caliber, talented legal personnel. In addition, he has proposed a series of important measures for training engineers, technical personnel in rural areas, writers and artists who have moral integrity and outstanding artistic excellence, and high-caliber administrators with both academic and technical expertise.

We must devote ourselves to improving people's lives. Meeting people's yearning for a better life is our goal and provides direction for education services. People-centered development is fundamental to upholding and developing Chinese socialism. As General Secretary Xi has pointed out, the Chinese Dream is ultimately people's dream. We must rely on the people to realize the Chinese Dream and improve their lives. Education must adhere to the people-centered philosophy. It must accompany each individual throughout his or her life. Likewise, it must be equal for everyone, more flexible, and more open, thus constantly increasing people's sense of gain from education and meeting their growing needs for a better life.

# 3. Education for Economic and Social Progress

Since the 18th CPC National Congress, China has made remarkable progress in education reform, development, and modernization. Education promotes economic and social growth while also making important contributions to social harmony and cultural prosperity. Xi Jinping pointed out at the National Education Conference that education should drive economic and social growth. This means that education must be more focused and versatile, and better adapted to economic and social development and the needs of the people.

## 3.1 Developing education in accordance with the Five-Sphere Integrated Plan and the Four-Pronged Comprehensive Strategy

Education should serve the Five-Sphere Integrated Plan. To develop the economy, the education sector must make greater contributions to its quality growth. Education must play a role in the implementation of the strategies of innovation-driven development, rural revitalization, and coordinated regional development. To promote socialist political progress, education should take the lead in improving democratic literacy and establishing a law-based system governing education and the establishment and management of schools. To strengthen socialist culture, the education sector should deepen research on Marxist theory, create a philosophy and social science system with Chinese characteristics, and ensure that Xi Jinping Thought on Socialism with Chinese Characteristics for a New Era takes root in the hearts of the people; it should also serve to develop a prosperous socialist culture that is national, scientific, and popular, and geared to modernization, the world, and the future. To advance social development, the education sector should contribute to social justice through equitable distribution of educational resources, participate in the Healthy China Initiative, and work with other sectors to create a social governance framework based on collaboration, participation, and benefit sharing. To promote ecological progress, education must play a crucial role in raising environmental awareness, disseminating the concept of sustainable development, and fostering the capacity to build a beautiful China.

Education should play an important role in the Four-Pronged Comprehensive Strategy. To secure a decisive victory in building a moderately prosperous society in all respects, we must rely on education as the fundamental policy for eliminating poverty and creating prosperity. We should work hard to ensure that every child has the opportunity to receive an education, and that all people can enjoy better and more equitable education. To achieve deeper reform, we need education to maximize consensus. We must keep moving in the right direction for comprehensively deepening reform, foster innovative talent, and modernize China's system and capacity for governance. To comprehensively promote law-based governance, we must, through education, strengthen our faith in following the path of the socialist rule of law with Chinese characteristics. We must intensify efforts to comprehensively popularize the law and raise people's awareness and knowledge of the rule of law. And we must vigorously train socialist legal talent. In an all-out effort to enforce strict Party discipline, we must strengthen all the members' awareness of Party principles through education, raise their political awareness and political abilities, build a force of high-caliber, specialized officials, and enhance their governance skills.

### 3.2 Strengthening the training of innovative and versatile talent

Different countries find themselves at different stages of development, and therefore their requirements for education and training also differ. The 18th CPC National Congress made important decisions about implementing an innovation-driven development strategy, and the 19th CPC National Congress further emphasized the need to accelerate the building of an innovative country. Being "innovation-driven" essentially means being "talent-driven," and thus people are the most critical factor in innovation. To accomplish extraordinary feats requires extraordinary persons.[1] Xi Jinping has pointed out that the time is right for innovation and for realizing our dreams. Procuring talent is the only route to success. The key to procuring talent is to broaden the pathways through which they are selected and trained, to allow them to improve their abilities, and to provide them with ample opportunities to apply their talents. Innovative undertakings call for innovative talent, who in turn rely on education and training. "To lead the world in scientific and technological innovation, China must discover talented individuals through the practice of innovation. It must train talent through innovation activities, and it must pool talent through undertakings in innovation. We must vigorously train a large and well-structured force of high-quality, innovative talent in science and technology."[2]

At present, China's structural shortage of innovative talent in science and technology is a prominent problem. There is a shortage of global leaders in science and technology. The training of talent in engineering and technology is out of synch with the needs of industry and innovation. There must be greater awareness and understanding of innovation, practical ability, and entrepreneurial spirit. In particular, the supply of innovative, practical, and interdisciplinary talent needed for economic transformation and upgrading is insufficient. It is, therefore, necessary to strengthen the cultivation of innovators, especially top-notch

---

1 Cited from *The History of the Han Dynasty* written by Ban Gu (32-92) of the Eastern Han dynasty (25-220).

2 Xi Jinping: *Speech at the 17th Meeting of the Members of the Chinese Academy of Sciences and the 12th Meeting of the Members of the Chinese Academy of Engineering*, Chinese edition, People's Publishing House, Beijing, 2014, p. 17.

ones. This requires us to improve the capacity of talent education and optimize its structure.

Training mechanisms should be improved in accordance with the need for talent growth. The future belongs to the young. Possessing a force of young, innovative talent gives a country vitality, and it is also where a country's hope for scientific and technological development resides. Through education we should foster scientific spirits in young people, cultivate their innovative thinking, tap into their potential, enhance their innovative abilities, and encourage them to surpass their predecessors' achievements. By so doing, we will provide a steady stream of support for the rejuvenation of the Chinese nation. Society at large should actively foster a sound atmosphere that encourages and embraces bold innovation. And it must also accelerate the formation of training mechanisms, employment mechanisms, incentive mechanisms, and competition mechanisms conducive to the emergence of a broad range of talent. Society at large should also cultivate a fertile ground for growing talent, allowing them to strike roots and thrive.

We must foster our own talent and attract those from other sources, and encourage society to identify, value, respect, and employ them. Xi Jinping has emphasized the need to recognize the importance of talent. We should seek such people with eagerness and treat them as if they were treasures. We should recommend them without sticking to fixed practices, and employ them to their fullest potential. Back when he worked in Zhengding county, Hebei province, Xi Jinping attached great importance to talent. In accordance with one of his proposals, three large-scale surveys of talent were carried out around the county in 1982, establishing Zhengding's first "library of talent." In November of the same year, relevant documents were issued assuring talented individuals that they could focus on their work and contribute their ideas. He wrote a call to the whole country titled "Nine Aspects of the Policies and Measures for Attracting Talent." In just over a year, the county brought in 46 talented individuals and recruited 257 scientists. Xi Jinping also sent out more than 100 invitation letters to experts and scholars across the country to set up the Zhengding Economic

Advisory Group. Among others, Hua Luogeng the mathematician and Yu Guangyuan the economist agreed to be part of the team. Various measures thereby served as boosters for the economic and social development of Zhengding county. In the new era, China's rejuvenation is even more reliant on our ability to identify, gather, and retain talent. We must put them to best use, accept them, and value their contributions. We must attract and pool talent from all areas—from within and outside the Party, and from both home and abroad—and we must strive to create good conditions in which everyone is eager to join their ranks, has the ability to do so, works hard to succeed, and exercises their skills to the full.

## 3.3 Revitalizing China's capacity for innovation and creativity through education

"If you can one day renovate yourself, do so from day to day, and let there be daily renovation."[1] Innovation is the soul and driver of a nation's progress and prosperity, and it is China's greatest national endowment. General Secretary Xi has said that education is essential for revitalizing China's capacity for innovation and creativity, and for realizing China's rejuvenation. Therefore, education must fully serve the innovation-driven development strategy.

China still faces many challenges in innovation and creation, with not yet a strong ability in independent innovation, especially originality. There has been no fundamental improvement in the situation in which core technologies in key fields are controlled by others. Xi Jinping has emphasized that experience has repeatedly taught us that key and core technologies cannot be asked for, purchased, or begged for. Only by mastering them ourselves can we truly compete and develop, and thus fundamentally safeguard our national security. We cannot rely on the achievements of others to improve our own science and

---

1 Cited from *The Great Learning*.

technology. And it is even more imperative that we avoid being a technological vassal of other countries, always following in their footsteps. We thus have no choice but to take the path of independent innovation.

---

### ⚜ Quote from Xi Jinping ⚜

Development is the first priority, talent is the first resource, and innovation, the first driving force.

—Speech during the deliberation of the Guangdong delegation at the First Session of the 13th National People's Congress, March 7, 2018

---

We should encourage scientists working in the education sector to take the lead in innovation. Xi Jinping has pointed out that implementing China's innovation-driven development strategy, building an innovative country, and providing strong scientific and technological support for the realization of the Two Centenary Goals are the missions of this era entrusted to China's science and technology workers. China must dedicate itself to advancing science and technology, and become a world center for science and innovation. Facing a new trend of innovation, major countries are looking for breakthroughs, and they are trying to seize opportunities for future economic, scientific, and technological development. This situation, this challenge, and this mission are pressing. We cannot fall behind in this great competition for scientific and technological innovation. We must catch up with our competitors and strive to surpass them. The vast array of science and technology workers in China must understand the trends, seize opportunities, confront problems, rise to challenges, head for the frontiers of world science and technology, lead the direction for scientific and technological development, and shoulder this heavy responsibility entrusted by history.

We should raise the level of our research and enhance the originality of innovation made in institutions of higher learning. Xi Jinping has noted that we should attach great importance to breakthroughs in original and basic theories. He has also stated that we should strengthen scientific infrastructure, ensure continuous progress in basic, systematic, and cutting-edge research and development, and increase the supply of original achievements through independent innovation. Similarly, we must actively integrate with and make good use of global innovation resources, while also participating in the construction and utilization of large-scale international scientific facilities, research bases and centers—selectively but with focus, based on the actual and development needs of China. Regarding scientific and technological development, we must identify strategic areas and priorities that are of overall importance and that are related to long-term development. We must promote collaborative and open innovation through efficient and rational allocation of resources, and build an efficient and powerful supply chain for generic key technologies, making major breakthroughs in key technologies, and keeping key technologies in our own hands. We must improve research, work faster to establish a discipline of philosophy and social sciences with Chinese characteristics, and develop new types of think tanks with distinctive Chinese features at institutions of higher learning.

We should comprehensively strengthen innovation at institutions of higher learning, and promote collaborative innovation between industries, universities, and research institutes. Xi Jinping has emphasized that implementing an innovation-driven development strategy is a systematic project. Only by combining scientific and technological achievements with the needs of the country, the people, and the market—and completing the "hat trick" of scientific research, experimental development, and promotion and application—can the value of innovation and that of innovation-driven development be realized. Science and technology must be integrated with social development. Thus, we must deepen cooperation among industries, universities, and research institutes, and address bottlenecks in the commercialization of research results. There must be deeper reform of research management systems along with the establishment of a market-oriented innovation system in which enterprises, universities, and research institutes are deeply integrated with enterprises playing the leading role. We should improve our research systems to stimulate innovation and better commercialize research achievements; we should explore the possibility to establish a full-chain, networked, and open collaborative innovation alliance that integrates industries, universities, researchers, and users.

We should give full play to the role of education in strengthening socialist culture with Chinese characteristics, and inspire the cultural creativity of the whole nation. In his report to the 19th CPC National Congress, Xi Jinping pointed out that we must develop a socialist culture with Chinese characteristics, inspire the cultural creativity of our whole nation, and develop a great socialist culture in China. Cultural innovation is an important part in a nation's overall innovation and creativity. In education, we should vigorously promote the best of traditional Chinese culture, carry forward China's revolutionary culture, develop an advanced socialist culture, and make greater contributions to improving China's soft power.

# Chapter 9

## High-Caliber Teachers: Hope of the Nation

The Communist Party of China and the Chinese government attach great importance to work concerning teachers. General Secretary Xi Jinping has recognized that teachers are of utmost importance and enhancing their performance is upmost in priority. Teachers are hailed by Xi Jinping as builders of the nation's "Dream Team." Accordingly, good teachers are measured against four criteria: they should have ideals and beliefs, moral integrity, knowledge, and compassion. To make teaching a great career choice, fostering public respect for the teaching profession and teachers is of major importance. Along these lines, Xi Jinping has addressed a series of key issues of theoretical and practical importance: why lend weight to team building of teachers, what to expect of teachers for the new era, and how to build a qualified body of teachers, laying down the fundamentals for enhancing the performance of teachers in the new era.

# 1. Teachers as the Root of Education and the Source of Its Vitality

To Xi Jinping, teachers, the foremost source of educational development, underpin the prosperity, rejuvenation, and wellbeing of the nation. Work concerning teachers underlines the advancement of a great modern socialist country, the success of education reform and development, and the cultivation of a new generation of capable young people who are well prepared to join the socialist cause.

> ───── ❧ *Quote from Xi Jinping* ❧ ─────
>
> It would be a blessing to have met a good teacher in your life; it would be the glory of a school to be lined with great teachers; it would be the beacon of our nation to have generations of excellent teachers.
>
> —Speech at the meeting with teachers and students of Beijing Normal University, September 9, 2014

## 1.1 Quality teachers as a prerequisite for national rejuvenation

Flourish it will for a nation that honors their educators.[1] Xi Jinping has pointed out, "The prosperity of our country, rejuvenation of our nation, and development of education are contingent on nurturing a

---

1 Cited from *Xunzi*. Xunzi (313-238 BC) was a philosopher in the Warring States Period (475-221 BC).

well-structured, high-quality professional body of teachers characterized by nobility, vitality, and expertise. And we need quantity too."[1]

Whereas talent is key to realizing the Chinese Dream, namely, the great rejuvenation of the Chinese nation, the nurturing of talent counts on teachers. That is the gravity teachers bear in actualizing the dream. Over the years, Chinese teachers have followed up on the CPC policy on education. They teach with love, knowledge, wisdom, and dedication. Generations of talent cultivated have testified to the contributions teachers have made to China's education as well as national development and rejuvenation. The new era calls for a greater pool of high-quality talent, whose growth depends on a high-quality teaching workforce. In other words, the composite strength and quality of our entire nation hinges on the overall quality of our teachers. To develop the nation through talent, we must first and foremost build the professional capabilities of teachers.

Teachers are pillars for cultural inheritance and transmission. The soul of a nation manifests through its culture. Progress in Chinese civilization for thousands of years, as well as modern advancement of China and its spiritual outlook, as General Secretary Xi has reiterated, is inextricably bound up with the character and talent of the Chinese people. The great national spirit—the spirit of creativity, solidarity, imagination, and relentless pursuit—which has been forged and maintained by the Chinese people, must continue to be promoted for generations to come. The endeavor of education, and that of teachers, are to build on past successes for the future. In a word, teachers play a fundamental role in the inheritance and development of fine traditional Chinese culture and the national spirit.

Teachers are pivotal in developing a learning society. With the advent of a knowledge economy, learning has become essential for people to survive and thrive. Young parents expect a good early education for

---

1 Xi Jinping: *Being a Good Teacher to the Satisfaction of the Communist Party of China and the People—Speech at the Meeting with Teachers and Students of Beijing Normal University*, Chinese edition, People's Publishing House, Beijing, 2014, p. 4.

their children; adults out of school look forward to more opportunities to recharge and continue learning; whereas senior citizens want to enrich themselves to lead a more fulfilling life. These trends are extending education from school to society, laying the ground for a lifelong learning system linking both formal and informal education, both general and vocational education, and both pre-service and in-service education. Teachers are an integral part of this system and play a key role in building our ideal learning society.

## 1.2 Teachers as the most crucial asset for educational development

In his letter to teachers across the country on Teachers' Day in 2013, Xi Jinping held that teachers are the root of education and the source of its vitality, who shoulder the mission of ensuring every child's healthy growth and satisfying people's expectations. This statement reaffirms teachers' crucial role in education.

Teachers are the prerequisite for high-quality education. The rapid emergence of innovators in China is inseparable from the contribution and dedication of Chinese teachers. In a sense, the qualifications of teachers determine the quality of education. First-rate teachers ensure first-rate education, which, in turn, nurtures first-rate talent. The standard to appraise a school is whether it has quality teachers. Students always want to go to a school, a place, or a country with dedicated and knowledgeable teachers skillful in instruction. Teachers are the key to educational progress and modernization. Enhancing the performance of teachers is an important means of addressing the imbalance and inadequacy of education so as to meet the educational needs of the people.

Teachers are drivers of education reform and innovation. Xi Jinping has pointed out that teachers must be the major actors in the new education thrust. He has encouraged teachers to be innovative, throw themselves into this undertaking, and contribute toward modernizing China's education to raise its international competitiveness. China's education reform is going deeper and deeper. As teachers are the main force of the reform and work in the front line of education, they know best the needs of students, the problems in education, and the necessity, importance, and urgency of education reform. Admittedly, no education reform can succeed without the acceptance, participation, dedication, and creativity of teachers. Teachers, therefore, bear a great responsibility in education reform, innovation, and development.

Teachers serve as the key to educational development in poverty-stricken areas. General Secretary Xi has called on Chinese teachers to pioneer poverty alleviation and contribute to the educational development of poor areas and to the growth of the next generation. In meeting the objective of building a moderately prosperous society in all respects by 2020, poverty-stricken areas constitute the toughest challenge, which must be resolved with urgency. To alleviate poverty, we should create education opportunities for children in poor areas. Good education for these children frees them from poverty, and moves them out of remote and mountainous areas to further their dreams. Fostering a team of teachers that meet the needs of the new era and the country is an urgent task and a visionary and strategic choice for the future.

## 1.3 Teachers as dream builders

Teachers shoulder the critical responsibility of nurturing the new generation for national rejuvenation. Xi Jinping has stressed that the mission of a teacher, as an engineer of the human soul, is to impart knowledge, disseminate the truth, shape lives, and prepare the young for the future. This observation is a profound illustration of the mission and responsibility endowed on teachers by the era. China is marching toward a moderately prosperous society in all respects and is on track in realizing the Chinese Dream of national rejuvenation. The Chinese Dream can only be realized by the generations with ideals, capability, and a strong sense of responsibility. The nurturing of such future generations mandates a community of high-quality teachers who are dream builders for them.

Teachers are beacons of light brightening the future of students.

Xi Jinping emphasized at the National Education Conference that teachers should guide students in character building, encourage learning and creative thinking, and act as their examples for devotion to the nation. "The root of goodness lies in education, and the root of education lies in teachers."[1] An unintentional utterance from a teacher may either inspire one to soar to greatness or suppress one's potential. Their work has a direct impact on the growth of young people, who are in a vital stage of developing scientific ways and skills of thinking. They need to be trained to analyze problems from correct positions and perspectives, and to think historically, dialectically, systematically, and creatively. Young people eagerly acquire knowledge, just as a sponge absorbs water. They are like a piece of jade waiting to be carved into a fine piece of work by their teachers. They should be helped to develop noble character and fine conduct.

## 2. Striving to Be Teachers Meeting the Expectations of the Party and the People

The cause of the CPC and the nation calls for a sizable pool of good teachers. Every teacher should improve his or her performance. Speaking to teachers and students of Beijing Normal University on the eve of Teachers' Day in 2014, Xi Jinping proposed four criteria for teachers. That is, they should have ideals and beliefs, moral integrity, knowledge, and compassion. He reiterated these criteria at a meeting with teachers and students of Peking University in 2018 and again, at the National Education Conference. These criteria have defined the new expectations and requirements for teachers in the new era.

---

1 Cited from *Elaboration on the Book of Potential Use* by Li Gou (1009-1059), a Chinese educator and philosopher in the Northern Song dynasty (960-1127).

## 2.1 Ideals and beliefs

Staying true to the long-term goal of communism and the shared ideal of socialism with Chinese characteristics is the foremost quality of a good teacher.

> ❦ *Quote from Xi Jinping* ❦
>
> Lofty ideals and beliefs guide teachers in cultivating students as seeds for the future.
>
> —Speech at the meeting with teachers and students of Beijing Normal University, September 9, 2014

A good teacher not only imparts knowledge but also cultivates ideals. Han Yu, a Tang-dynasty scholar, said, "A teacher communicates beliefs, imparts knowledge, and clears confusion." It is the foremost mission of a teacher to cultivate ideals, and those who only impart knowledge and answer questions are not good enough. Good teachers are expected to take the cultivation of ideals as their number one mission and responsibility. Teachers are guardians of civilization and the guides of students. A dream is ignited by another dream and an ideal is inspired by another ideal. A teacher with ideals can sow the seeds of dreams in students. In an era with increasingly diversified values, teachers should lead students forward with great ambitions, pure souls, and noble sentiment on the basis of lofty ideals and convictions.

Good teachers should bear the mission for society and the nation in their heart. Virtually all good teachers who are remembered in history worked for the future of the nation. In December 2017, Xi Jinping issued an instruction in response to a letter from 15 senior professors of Xi'an Jiaotong University, saluting the veteran professors who had answered the call of the government and devoted themselves to the reconstruction of northwest China. He encouraged teachers and students of the university to carry on the fine spirit of this group of long-serving professors in contributing their wisdom and strength. In his 2018 New Year Message, he again referred to these veteran professors, acclaiming their patriotism and devotion.

Today, a good teacher should stand with the Party and the people, study Xi Jinping Thought on Socialism with Chinese Characteristics for a New Era, stay true to socialism with Chinese characteristics, enhance his or her confidence in China's socialist path, theory, system, and culture, and guide his or her students in loving the nation, the people, and the Party. If a teacher chooses a career of cultivating talent for national development and rejuvenation, and takes pleasure in doing so, then his or her life will be endowed with eternal values, and this career will take on great significance.

### 2.2 Moral integrity

"A teacher should teach students not only skills but also ethical values."[1] Xi Jinping emphasizes that teachers must be people of moral integrity. "Those who cannot tell good from evil, right from wrong, justice from injustice, or gain from loss, are not good teachers."[2]

---

### ⟨ Quote from Xi Jinping ⟩

Apart from their knowledge and ability, teachers also influence their students through personal conduct and the values they hold toward the country, the people, the public, and the private.

—Speech at the meeting with teachers and students of Beijing Normal University, September 9, 2014

---

1 Cited from *The Book of Rites*, which was an important Confucian classic in the Western Han dynasty (206 BC–25 AD).
2 Xi Jinping: *Being a Good Teacher to the Satisfaction of the Communist Party of China and the People—Speech at the Meeting with Teachers and Students of Beijing Normal University*, Chinese edition, People's Publishing House, Beijing, 2014, p. 6.

Moral integrity is an important standard that teachers should meet in performing their duties. Xi Jinping has noted that the professional nature of teachers determines that they should be models of moral integrity. Good teachers should set up a good example by teaching and behaving ethically. They are a mirror of moral conduct to students. As a saying goes, "Teachers are models of good conduct."[1] What they say and do are taken as norms and emulated by their students. If teachers transgress the moral line, they will mislead the students and adversely affect the formation of their beliefs. *The Analects* also states, "A man commands with his integrity."[2] Students not only listen to what teachers say, but also observe what they do. As teachers are models in the eyes of their students, they need to aim high and keep improving their moral conduct to equal the virtuous, thus becoming master teachers who may mold the students' character, behavior, and taste.

A teacher's moral conduct needs to be improved through self-cultivation. As Xi Jinping has emphasized, "A teacher's moral conduct should be improved through education and, more importantly, through self-cultivation. Teachers must constantly strive to be noble-minded and resist vulgar interests. They should be selfless and devote their heart and soul to teaching. They should adhere to their ideals and be morally incorruptible. They should take the lead in promoting socialist ethics and traditional Chinese virtues and be models for students."[3] Teachers' moral integrity reflects their intellectual accomplishment and cultural taste. As the saying goes, "A refined character comes from extensive reading." Teachers need to read good books to cultivate noble character. They also need to practice what they preach. They should set strict standards for themselves and demonstrate through action their proper understanding of the relationship between the self, the state, and the people.

---

1 Cited from "Translating Learning into Action" of *Model Sayings* by Yang Xiong (53 BC–18 AD), an educator and philosopher in the Western Han dynasty (206 BC–25 AD).
2 Cited from "Zilu" of *The Analects.*
3 Xi Jinping: *Being a Good Teacher to the Satisfaction of the Communist Party of China and the People—Speech at the Meeting with Teachers and Students of Beijing Normal University,* Chinese edition, People's Publishing House, Beijing, 2014, p. 7.

They need to, as Confucius put it in *The Analects*, "reflect on themselves three times a day" and constantly strive to equal the virtuous. Only in this way can they appreciate and demonstrate the appeal of noble character and become moral paragons for students.

Good teachers love their career. As is often said, you should love whatever job you take up. A good teacher should not take teaching just as a means to raise the family. As Xi Jinping has pointed out, only those who are engaged in education as a cause can do it well. Those who are physically at school but actually aim to climb the social ladder or make monetary profits may ultimately surrender their nobility to money and/or fame. These people cannot make good teachers. A dedicated person devotes wholly and earnestly to his or her purpose. Only those who are dedicated to education will love their students, be strict with themselves, rigorous in research, and tireless in teaching, thus becoming role models of their students. Only such teachers will engage in life-long learning, pursue constant progress, and lead themselves and their students to success. Xi Jinping has stressed, "The greatest success for a teacher is to bring out the best in their students. Consider how reassured and proud the teachers are when they see their students grow to be learned, well mannered, well established, and happy."[1] In the new era, many outstanding teachers have come to the fore. They are dedicated to their career, live a simple life, and never flinch in the face of difficulties. With devotion and passion, they help their students realize their dreams. They are indeed models of all other teachers, who should resist material temptations, always put their students first, and take imparting knowledge and cultivating moral character as their lifelong pursuit.

## 2.3 Knowledge

Teachers have been acclaimed as "sages" since ancient times. Good

---

1 Xi Jinping: *Being a Good Teacher to the Satisfaction of the Communist Party of China and the People—Speech at the Meeting with Teachers and Students of Beijing Normal University*, Chinese edition, People's Publishing House, Beijing, 2014, p. 8.

teachers should have solid knowledge because "Shallow water cannot lift a big ship."[1] General Secretary Xi Jinping emphasizes that teachers should champion learning. They are expected to be knowledgeable, competent, diligent, and good at teaching.

Good teachers are well-grounded in knowledge and have broad horizons and vision. Otherwise, they will feel stretched and never be able to accomplish the job with ease. In-depth knowledge in specific areas and pedagogy is the prerequisite and foundation for teaching. Teachers are expected to draw on their knowledge in teaching, know their students' potential well, be effective in their teaching approaches, and help their students learn faster and better. In the information era, they should know much more than what is needed for teaching. They should have both solid domain knowledge, a wide range of general knowledge, and a broad mind and vision. They should have the wisdom to learn, to get on with others, to live a meaningful life, and to educate. They not only give fish but also teach how to fish, and they should guide and help students in all respects.

---

### ⟬∽Quote from Xi Jinping∽⟭

In the past, we believed that teachers should have a bucket of water before they can give students a bowl of water. This is not enough today, as they should have a pond of water before they can give students a bowl of water.

—Speech at the meeting with teachers and students of Beijing Normal University, September 9, 2014

---

A good teacher should pursue lifelong learning. With the rapid progression of information technology and economic globalization, people are expected to have greater flexibility, adaptability, initiative, team spirit,

---

1 Cited from "Free and Easy Wondering" by Zhuang Zhou (*c.* 369-286 BC), a philosopher and writer in the Warring States Period (475-221 BC).

and innovative skills, and this places higher demands on teachers. Therefore, they should keep learning, acquire frontier knowledge, work hard, and constantly improve and enrich themselves. Teachers should advance with the times, pursue excellence, and meet new challenges proactively. Only in this way can they both continuously improve themselves and prepare students for the future.

Good teachers should have a strong innovative mindset. Xi Jinping has noted that education aims to equip students with practical skills and innovative spirit. Teachers in China should be creative in developing a first-class and modern education system with Chinese characteristics. Teachers' awareness and ability of innovation are of great significance to talent cultivation and educational development. Innovation-minded teachers are self-motivated to build their capabilities for better delivery quality. Their teaching is informed by new knowledge on education and cutting-edge research outcomes, and profits from scientific and efficient teaching approaches. They are capable of guiding their students in making critical inquiry so as to turn them into pillars of the nation with extensive knowledge, a broad vision, moral integrity, and professional competence.

## 2.4 Compassion

Xi Jinping has pointed out that good teachers emanate compassion. Teachers may teach in different ways, but they should have something in common: love for their students.

### ❧ *Quote from Xi Jinping* ❧

Education is a profession founded on love and compassion. Love is the soul of education, without which, there would be no education.

—Speech at the meeting with teachers and students of Beijing Normal University, September 9, 2014

Good teachers are loving and trustful. They care about all students, boost their confidence through appreciation, and build up their dignity through trust. They make sure that all students achieve healthy growth and enjoy success. They know when to be strict and when to be lenient. They reason with students and move students with affection, so that students trust them and believe in what they say. Love is the gate to knowledge and enlightenment. Love nurtures beautiful hearts. Being loving, truthful, and sincere, good teachers foster, inspire, and spread love, forge emotional bonds with students, and become their close friends.

Compassion begets responsibility. Good teachers know that when choosing this career, they shoulder important responsibilities, that is, imparting knowledge, educating students, and fostering their moral integrity. They are expected to perform these responsibilities in their everyday work. Teachers' sense of responsibility determines their achievements. It is their love for education and students that sustains their lifelong dedication to their career, and gives them the courage to stand up when their students are in danger and the determination to make breakthroughs in studies.

A good teacher respects and understands students. As General Secretary Xi has put it, without respect, understanding, and compassion, there will be no education to speak of. Good teachers fill students with confidence and teach them to respect others by showing respect for them. Everyone, children and adolescents in particular, wants to be respected and cared about. A teacher should, as Confucius said, "continue study without respite and instruct others without growing weary"[1] and no one should be denied education. Just as we cannot find two tree leaves exactly the same in the world, students have different characters, habits, temperaments, interests, family backgrounds, and abilities. Teachers should adopt approaches suited to their students' abilities and conditions, and they should never show indifference or play favorites. Moreover, they must not label students as "good" or "bad" ones. They should try even

---

1 Cited from "Shu Er" of *The Analects*.

harder to understand and help low achievers or problem students with care and compassion. Good teachers should treat their students as equals, respect them, understand their sentiments, find out their strengths, and tolerate their shortcomings, so as to bring out their full potential.

## 3. Building a Body of Qualified and Professional Teachers

At the National Education Conference, Xi Jinping affirmed the need to improve the professional competence of our teachers. Since the 18th CPC National Congress, he has made several speeches about the importance of this issue, emphasizing that we should take it as the most important task in education and that we should strengthen the professional ethics and moral integrity of teachers and foster public respect for teachers so that teaching will become a profession admired by all.

### 3.1 Prioritizing professional ethics in evaluating teachers' performance

Xi Jinping attaches great importance to enhancing professional ethics and integrity of Chinese teachers. He once pointed out, "Professional ethics and integrity are the most important criteria for appraising the performance of teachers."[1] Teachers' moral and political integrity and their professional conduct determine what kind of people their students will become, which is crucial for the future of the nation and should therefore be given top priority. Core socialist values should be integrated into the entire course of imparting knowledge and cultivating people. All teachers must observe professional ethics. They should spread

---

1 Xi Jinping: *Speech at the Meeting with Teachers and Students of Peking University,* Chinese edition, People's Publishing House, 2018, p. 9.

advanced thought and culture, support the governance by the Party, and work to promote well-rounded development of students.

To strengthen professional ethics and integrity, the Four Integrations must be carried out. In December 2016, at the National Conference on Moral and Political Work in Institutions of Higher Learning, Xi Jinping pointed out, "We must strengthen our teachers' ethics and standards, so that they integrate education with moral cultivation, teach by word and deed, devote their attention to both research and social issues, and adhere to academic ethics while enjoying academic freedom."[1] To carry out both instruction and moral cultivation, we should encourage teachers to teach in a caring way with students' character and age in mind. In every class, they should impart not only knowledge but also values so that what they teach will enhance students' physical and mental health. Schools should also ensure that all students receive sincere care and help, so that the seeds of core socialist values take root and grow in their hearts.

To integrate teaching by word with teaching by deed, teachers should be encouraged to observe professional ethical norms, dedicate themselves to their job, and be the role model for their students. In this way, their professional conduct can influence students. To integrate dedication to research with attention to social issues, teachers should be guided to gain a better understanding of reality and love both their families and our country. In this way, they can attain a deeper understanding of the Communist Party of China, the country, and society, and thus conduct research in the interests of society. To integrate observing academic ethics with enjoying academic freedom, teachers should be guided to perform their duties and abide by academic norms and ethics so as to safeguard justice and ensure an academic atmosphere of professional integrity. The Four Integrations must be carried out as the overarching principles guiding teachers' conduct, teaching, and research.

---

1 Xi Jinping: *The Governance of China*, Vol. II, Foreign Languages Press, Beijing, 2017, p. 409.

To strengthen professional ethics and integrity of teachers requires both guidance and self-cultivation. General Secretary Xi has noted, "Preachers must have a thorough understanding of and a firm faith in what they preach. University and college teachers should first receive education themselves..."[1] Teachers should combine knowledge impartation with self-cultivation. They should apply high ethical standards in their conduct, academic studies, and teaching, and such standards should be incorporated in the training and management of teachers. All teachers should study and gain a full understanding of Xi Jinping Thought on Socialism with Chinese Characteristics for a New Era, and imbue themselves with lofty beliefs and ideals. They should learn the best of traditional Chinese culture to cultivate their professional ethics and carry forward traditional ethics through teaching. They should develop self-discipline, identify themselves with their profession, defend its dignity and reputation, and constantly improve their ethical standards. The cultivation of professional ethics should have an important place in the career plan of teachers, who should improve themselves through learning, internalize professional ethics, and externalize them in their daily life and work.

We should keep fostering professional ethics and integrity in teachers, and strict standards should be set and regular supervision be exercised. Professional ethics should be demonstrated, and supporting policies, institutions, and laws be instituted. A professional ethics development mechanism featuring education, communication, assessment, supervision as well as rewards and sanctions should be put in place. This will enable teachers to respect, discipline, and strengthen themselves and become instructors on character building and learning, pacesetters of observing socialist ethics and professional conduct, and champions of fairness and justice.

Xi Jinping has pointed out that we must not fail to see that there are still problems with some teachers, which should be taken seriously and resolved. Those individuals who have become morally degenerate

---

1  Xi Jinping: *The Governance of China*, Vol. II, Foreign Languages Press, Beijing, 2017, p. 409.

or broken the law must be expelled and punished in accordance with the law. There must be zero-tolerance for abusing students.

## 3.2 Improving the teacher education system with Chinese characteristics

Training of teachers underpins the cause of education. Since the 18th CPC National Congress, Xi Jinping has emphasized on many occasions that education should start with teacher training. The teacher education system should be strengthened to improve training quality.

It is important to increase support for teacher education. Xi Jinping has noted, "We should identify major problems in the training of teachers, adopt forceful steps to deepen reform, and continue to improve the training of teachers."[1] For some time, the teacher education system in some places has not performed well, and there has been insufficient support for teacher training institutions. Some teachers fail to meet the need for cultivating talent in the new era in terms of competence, and their moral and political standards and professional ethics need to be raised. Xi Jinping has emphasized that CPC committees and governments at all levels and authorities concerned must attach great importance to training teachers, improve training institutions, and build an open and integrated training system. This system should be primarily composed of dedicated teacher training institutions and supported by high-standard non-teacher training institutions, with high-standard kindergartens as well as primary and secondary schools serving as places for interns.[2] It is necessary to increase input in teacher training and improve the funding system with governmental input as the key source supplemented by multi-source funds. Capacity to train teachers should

---

1 Xi Jinping: *Being a Good Teacher to the Satisfaction of the Communist Party of China and the People—Speech at the Meeting with Teachers and Students of Beijing Normal University*, Chinese edition, People's Publishing House, Beijing, 2014, p. 13.
2 "*China Education Modernization 2035* issued by the CPC Central Committee and the State Council," *People's Daily*, February 24, 2019.

be increased, standards should be set for teacher training institutions, and a number of teacher training bases should be established, so as to improve the overall performance of teacher training institutions and departments.

It is important to enhance training in a systematic way and enable teachers to gain practical experience. High-performing teachers themselves have been trained by high-caliber teachers. Therefore, equal emphasis should be placed on both teachers' pre-service training and on-the-job training, so as to enhance their career development. Lifelong learning should also be encouraged. Top-level teachers should play an exemplary and leading role and help other teachers put their heart into teaching and research instead of fame and wealth hunt. A favorable environment should be created so that young teachers could grow rapidly. We should promote teaching reform and innovation and encourage teachers and administrators to explore new ideas, models, and approaches, to form a characteristic teaching and education style, and to create systems and environments conducive to producing great educators.

### 3.3 Raising teachers' social status

The Chinese nation has always had great respect for teachers, placed great value on education, and held wisdom and learning in great reverence. In 1999, when he was Deputy Secretary of the CPC and Acting Governor of Fujian province, Xi Jinping wrote back to Chen Qiuying, his teacher of Chinese language at junior middle school, saying, "Public respect for teachers and public support for education is a traditional virtue of the Chinese people. As Chairman Mao said to his teacher Xu Teli, 'Once my teacher, you will be my teacher forever.' I will never forget your kindness." In 2016, on the eve of the thirty-second Teachers' Day, Xi Jinping went to see the teachers and students of Beijing Bayi School where he had studied. He invited Chen Qiuying and Chen Zhonghan, who had taught him, as well as the family members of the late teachers who had taught him, to attend the meeting with teachers and students of the school. Hearing the headmaster address him as Chief, Xi humbled himself, "I am no leader here, but a student." One of the teachers remarked, "You always have schools, teachers, and students in your heart." To this Xi replied, "Because it is teachers who educate us." His words moved the audience. Xi Jinping himself sets a good example in appreciating teachers and valuing education.

At the National Education Conference, General Secretary Xi Jinping pointed out that the Party and the public should foster a culture that engenders respect for teachers and promotes education so as to raise the political, social, and professional status of teachers. To improve their political status, we should ensure their rights and opportunities for political participation. To improve their social status, we should accord teachers due recognition and respect in their educational role. To improve their professional status, we should make teaching an appealing profession and fill teachers with a sense of achievement.

---

### ◈ Quote from Xi Jinping ◈

The CPC committees and governments at all levels should care about teachers, so that they can enjoy teaching free of concerns. We should see that they have a sense of achievement and honor and make teaching a profession admired by all.

—Speech during his visit to Beijing Bayi School, September 9, 2016

---

To raise teachers' status, we should better their pay packages. Xi Jinping emphasized at the National Education Conference that as school conditions improve, more input in education should be used for bettering the lives of teachers so that they can focus on teaching. A sustainable pay adjustment mechanism should be established to ensure pay raise of primary and secondary school teachers. A salary structure for college teachers should also be set up to incentivize initiatives by teachers to add value to knowledge.

Xi Jinping has paid special attention to the wellbeing of teachers in rural and poverty-stricken areas, and he has stressed the importance of offering incentives to encourage young teachers to work in those areas. At a Central Conference on Ethnic Affairs, he noted, "Basic working and living conditions must be secured for teachers. More attention must be given to those working in border and rural areas. More education funding from the central government should be channeled to ethnic minority areas and border areas. We must pursue this as a long-term goal."[1] At the National Education Conference, he reiterated that rural teachers are pivotal to developing rural education, and for that reason, preferential treatments should be offered to encourage them to stay on their jobs; and more opportunities should be created for their career advancement.

To raise teachers' status, it is important to foster public respect for teachers. Xi Jinping has called on the entire society to realize the importance and specialness of teaching and make respect for teachers a social ethos. Culture carries the national spirit and forges social consensus. The culture of respecting teachers should be highlighted. The government, the public, schools, and families should work together to accord more respect to teachers and keep alive the Chinese tradition of valuing education, honoring teachers, and prizing learning. Respect for teachers should be a key part of our education on Chinese culture and core socialist values, and every child should be taught to respect their teachers through classroom teaching as well as campus and public activities. We should establish a national honor system for teachers to award outstanding teachers, and eulogize Role Models of the Times and Teachers of the Year.

To raise the status of teachers, CPC committees and governments at all levels should fulfil their respective missions and responsibilities. They should be aware of the importance of teachers from a strategic perspective and place teachers in the center of educational development. Priority should be given to teachers' affairs, inputs for teachers,

---

1 Party Literature Research Office of the CPC Central Committee: *Excerpts of Xi Jinping's Discourses on Socialist Society Construction*, Chinese edition, Central Party Literature Press, 2017, p. 52.

and teachers' team building. Major decisions of the CPC and the state on strengthening the ranks of teachers should be fully implemented. Teachers' professional development must be supported and the problems they encounter must be solved, so as to enable them to live a secure and respectable life. It is important to improve management of teachers and services for them, better the qualification and certification systems, deepen reform of the professional title system, optimize management of teaching posts, and remove institutional barriers to keep teachers fully motivated and inspire their creativity.

# Compilers' Postscript

*Understanding Xi Jinping's Educational Philosophy* was compiled under the auspices of the Ministry of Education (MOE) of the People's Republic of China and approved by the National Textbook Committee Office. The contents of the manuscript were verified by the Institute of Party History and Literature of the CPC Central Committee, and the pictures were provided by Xinhua News Agency and China Media Group. The manuscript was then reviewed by the four research centers (institutes) for Xi Jinping Thought on Socialism with Chinese Characteristics for a New Era affiliated to the Ministry of Education, Peking University, Tsinghua University, and Renmin University of China. Besides, opinions and suggestions were solicited from education departments at all levels, as well as from the faculty, staff, and students of primary and secondary schools and institutions of higher education.

Under the direct leadership of MOE Minister Chen Baosheng and with the specific guidance of Vice Minister Zheng Fuzhi, MOE's Department of National Textbook organized the editing and reviewing of this book. Yang Xiaohui was the compilation team leader. The team members included Ai Silin, Fan Guorui, Gao Deyi, Pang Lisheng, Qin Xuan, Shen Wenhua, Shi Zhongying, Sun Xiguo, Wan Meirong, Wang Binglin, Wang Zhanren, Yang Yinfu, Yang Zhaoshan, Zhai Xiaoning, and Zhang Qingshou. Other members included Li Yan, Kang Xiuyun, Gao Di, Zhang Haibo, Liu Zhi, Li Yayuan, Yan Weigang, Duan Yan, Qu Bo, and Zhang Zeqiang. Experts who reviewed the book were Gu Hailiang, Wang Ronghua, Yang He, Hu Shuxiang, Xie Weihe, Zhang Li, Zhang Guozuo, and Zheng Shiqu, among others.

October 2019

# Translators' Postscript

The translation of *Understanding Xi Jinping's Educational Philosophy* was commissioned to Beijing Foreign Studies University (BFSU) by the National Textbook Committee Office, and the project includes versions in English, French, Russian, Spanish, and Arabic. Beijing Foreign Studies University established a university-level coordinating group led by Professor Wang Dinghua and Professor Sun Youzhong in order to ensure the successful completion of the project as scheduled.

Professor Ren Wen led the English translation team, whose main members included Li Changshuan, Peng Ping, Tham Wai Mun (from Singapore), Zhai Zheng, Zhu Yuben, Liu Yubo, Liu Moxiao, and Eliot I. Wycoff (from the United States). David W. Ferguson (from the United Kingdom) served as the English language editor.

With the guidance and support of the National Textbook Committee Office and the university-level coordinating group, the English translation team was able to navigate the challenges of time constraints and complete the translation and editing work by the end of 2021. We would thus like to express our heartfelt thanks to all institutions and individuals who worked tirelessly toward this goal. Readers are welcome to provide comments and suggestions on this translation.

December 21, 2021